A *Lagom* Guide to Swedish
– A *Say it in Swedish* book –

Joakim Andersson

NORTH TONE MEDIA

Paperback ISBN 978-91-987189-0-4
ePub ISBN 978-91-987189-1-1
PDF ISBN 978-91-987189-2-8

First edition
© 2021 Joakim Andersson, Say it in Swedish & North Tone Media
www.sayitinswedish.com
www.northtonemedia.com
North Tone Media Handelsbolag, Sweden
Author: Joakim Andersson

Contents

Foreword 15

How to Use This Book 17

The Basics 21

1   Nouns 21
2   Grammatical genders 21
3   The Swedish indefinite form 21
4   The Swedish definite form 22
5   Double definite 22
6   Plurals 23
7   Plurals with *-or* 23
8   Plurals with *-ar* 23
9   Plurals with *-er* 24
10   Plurals with *-r* 24
11   *En* word plurals without a suffix 24
12   *Ett* word plurals 24
13   The definite plural form 25
14   Uncountable nouns 25
15   Countable nouns as uncountables 26
16   Nouns without an article (*nakna substantiv*) 26
17   The possessive case with *-s* 26
18   The possessive case with prepositions 26
19   Compounds 26
20   Verbs in the first conjugation group 28
21   Verbs in the second conjugation group 28
22   Verbs in the third conjugation group 29

23 Verbs in the fourth conjugation group 30

24 Irregular verbs 31

25 Past tense 31

26 Perfect 32

27 Past perfect 33

28 Future tense 33

29 Future tense with *skola* 33

30 Future tense with *komma (att)* 34

31 Future tense with *tänka* 34

32 Reflexive verbs 34

33 Verb with reflexive features 34

34 Passive voice 35

35 Deponent verbs 35

36 False passives 36

37 Verbs with deponent features 37

38 Particle verbs 38

39 Helper verbs 39

40 Subjunctive mood 42

41 Past subjunctive mood 42

42 Adjectives 43

43 Adjectives (additional notes) 43

44 Comparing adjectives with suffixes 44

45 Comparing adjectives with *mer/mest* 44

46 Irregular adjectives 45

47 The third degree of adjective comparison 45

48 Indeclinable adjectives 46

49 Participle 46

50 Past participle 47

51 Adverbs 47

52 Locative adverbs 48

53	List of important adverbs	49
54	Question words, interrogative adverbs	51
55	Prepositions	51
56	List of important prepositions	52
57	Personal pronouns	54
58	Possessive pronouns	55
59	Reflexive pronouns	56
60	Reflexive possessive pronouns	57
61	Demonstrative pronouns	57
62	List of important pronouns	58
63	Conjunctions	60
64	Subjunctions	61
65	Numbers	62
66	Ordinal numbers	64

Pronunciation Secrets		66
67	Standard Swedish	66
68	Hard and soft vowels	66
69	Vowel qualities	67
70	The importance of *å*, *ä*, and *ö*	69
71	*Viby-i* (compressed, buzzing *i*)	69
72	*Viby-y*	70
73	The tenth vowel (*ô*)	70
74	When /ö/ becomes /u/	71
75	Diphthongization	71
76	When /ä/ becomes /e/	72
77	Shortened long /u/	72
78	Consonants	73
79	Consonants with letter combinations	73
80	The *tje* sound	74

81	The *sje* sound	74
82	Retroflex consonants	76
83	The letter *r*	77
84	Hard and soft *k* and *g*	78
85	Soft *g*	80
86	The *j* sound in letter combinations	80
87	Aspiration	80
88	*Tjockt l* (thick *l*)	81
89	The quantity rule	81
90	Long consonants	81
91	Stress	83
92	Pitch accents	83
93	The melodic accent	84
94	What are reductions?	85
95	Omission of endings	85
96	Omission of sounds in the middle of a word	86
97	Reduction of the definite *en* word ending	87
98	The definite plural *-en* in colloquial Swedish	87
99	Reduction of *-ig* in adjectives	88
100	Reduction of *-skt* in adjectives	88
101	Omission of verb endings	88
102	Omission of *-r*	89
103	Omission of *h-*	89
104	Assimilation	89
105	*N* + plosives	90
106	When /d/ becomes /r/	90
107	*Dom*	91
108	The pronunciation of *är*	91
109	*Och* and *att*	91
110	The pronunciation of *-or*	92

111 The pronunciation of numbers 92

112 *Vilken, vilket, vilka* 93

113 *Sicken, sicket, sicka* 93

114 Rule breaking words 94

115 The pronunciation of *stod* 95

Confusing Things 96

116 Prepositions, prepositions, prepositions 96

117 *På* 96

118 *I* 100

119 *Om* 103

120 *Mot/emot* 105

121 *Från/ifrån* 106

122 *Av/utav* and *i/uti* 106

123 How to tell *en* and *ett* words apart 107

124 Nouns with multiple genders 109

125 The uses of *den/det* 110

126 English loans with *-s* 111

127 The general *det* 111

128 Omission of *ha* 113

129 Omission of *som* 113

130 Omission of the main verb with *skola/måste* 114

131 *Skola (ska/skulle)* 114

132 *Få* 115

133 *Böra (borde)* 118

134 *Kunna* 118

135 Shortened verbs (*lägga, säga*) 119

136 Archaic shortened verbs (*hava, bliva*, etc.) 119

137 Unexpected past tense 120

138 *Stå, ligga, sitta* 120

139 *Ställa, lägga, sätta* 120

140 Weak and strong variants of the same verb 121

141 Replying to questions (*jo/nej*) 122

142 Replying to statements (*ja/nej*) 122

143 Semantic plural 123

144 The placement of *inte* (the *biff* rule) 124

145 Doubling words for emphasis 125

146 *Också/heller* 126

147 The weirdness of *egen* 126

148 *Blå/grå* vs. *blåa/gråa* 127

149 Defective adjectives 128

150 *Våran, vårat, eran,* and *erat* 129

151 *Liten, små, lilla* 129

152 *Lite* 130

153 *Annan, andra, till* 130

Old Swedish Relics 132

154 *Till* and the possessive case 132

155 *Han* vs. *honom* 133

156 Shortened pronouns (*'an* and *'na*) 133

157 *Å* vs. *på* 133

158 Set phrases in the present subjunctive 134

159 More on the past subjunctive 134

160 *Bli* vs. *varda* 135

161 Personal verb conjugations 135

162 Masculine in modern Swedish 136

163 The good old accusative 137

164 The good old dative 138

Mistakes Even Swedes Make 139

165 *Vart* instead of *var* 139

166 *Även fast* – a Frankenstein's monster 139

167 *Innan* vs. *före* 139

168 The "polite" pronoun 140

169 (Un)countable nouns with *mycket/lite* and *många/få* . . 141

170 Wrong comparison of *dålig* 142

171 *Eftersom att* 142

172 The dying reflexive pronoun 142

173 *Apropå* vs. *att bero på* 143

174 *Än* – a preposition or a subjunction? 143

Polite Swedish 144

175 Swedes aren't rude 144

176 *Tack* and polite requests 144

177 Requests with *skulle* 145

178 *Snälla* 146

179 Formal requests with *vänligen* 146

180 Swedes and thanking 146

181 How to reply to thanks 146

182 The lack of a polite pronoun 147

Vocabulary 148

183 *Gå* does not mean *to go* 148

184 *Lära sig* 148

185 *Ihjäl* – doing something to death 149

186 *Leka, spela* 149

187 *Kille/tjej, flicka/pojke* 150

188 *Kaka, kex* 151

189 *Saft, juice* 151

190 *Prova, pröva* – an umlaut makes the difference 151

191 *Tänka, tycka, tro* – it's not what you think 152

192 *Tycka* 153

193 *Tro* 153

194 *Varmt* is hot 153

195 *Spendera, tillbringa* 154

196 *Smärre* 154

197 *Timma/timme, trappa/trapp, ända/ände* 155

198 *Gilla, tycka om* 155

199 *Handla, köpa* 156

200 *Sista, senaste* 157

201 *Människa, person, folk* 158

202 *Person* 159

203 *Folk* 159

204 *Köra* 160

205 How to compare *dålig, ond*, and *illa* 160

206 *Värre, värst* 161

207 *Illa* 161

208 Family members (maternal/paternal) 162

209 More special family members 162

210 *Pojkvän, flickvän* vs. *killkompis, tjejkompis* 163

211 *Minnas* vs. *komma ihåg* 163

212 *Glömma (bort)* 164

213 *Bredvid* and *jämte* 165

214 *Långsamt, snabbt* vs. *sakta, fort* 165

215 *Simma, bada* 166

216 *Antingen eller, varken eller, vare sig eller* 166

217 *Varken eller, vare sig eller* 167

218 *Trivas* 167

219 *Passa på* – an essential Swedish word 168

220 *Duktig* 169

X

221 Untranslatable Swedish words 170

222 Words specific to Sweden 170

FAQ & Common Pitfalls 174

223 The V2 word order 174

224 Mentioning one's country of origin 174

225 *Eftersom* 175

226 *Därför att* 175

227 *För att* 176

228 *För* (conjunction) 177

229 *Till*, *åt*, and *för* 177

230 *Till* 178

231 *Åt* 178

232 *Hej* and *hallå* 179

233 Formal and colloquial greetings 179

234 Writing compounds apart – a deadly sin 180

235 *Må* 181

236 *Båda*, *både* and *bägge* 181

237 *God* or *bra*? 182

238 *Heta* – My name is 184

239 *Mena* vs. *betyda* 184

240 *Känna (till)* 185

241 Centuries 185

242 *På* or *i svenska*? 186

Tips, Fun Facts & Good-To-Knows 187

243 Create your own verb 187

244 Turning verbs into nouns 187

245 Fake diminutive with *-is* 187

246 Slang words with *-o* 191

247 *É* in Swedish 192

248 Opposites with *o-* 192

249 Independant opposites 193

250 Nominal phrases 194

251 *Göra* (to do) as a placeholder 194

252 Omission of "people" 195

253 Different ways to say *yes* and *no* 195

254 *Oj* and *nämen* 196

255 Replace *mycket* for *väldigt* and *jätte-* 198

256 Defective verbs 198

257 The present tense as an imperative 199

258 Passive voice with *-s* 199

259 Passive voice with *bli* 202

260 Present participle with *-s* 204

261 Exclusion of possessive pronouns 204

262 *Ju* 204

263 *Nog* 205

264 *Väl* 205

265 The question tag *eller hur* 205

266 *Va?* 206

267 *Eller?* 206

268 A kind of present continuous tense 206

269 *Din idiot!* 208

270 *Vad kul!* 209

271 Swedish likes its verbs 209

272 *Alltså, liksom,* and *ba* – annoying (?) fillers 209

273 *Liksom* 210

274 *Ba* 210

275 *En annan* – I'm someone else 210

276 *Tills, medans, förräns,* and *tillbaks* 211

277 Addressing one person with the plural *ni* 211

278 Seeking attention with *du* 212

279 *Hörrö, sörrö* 212

280 Elfdalian (*Älvdalska*) 213

281 The Scandinavian languages 213

282 Norwegian 215

283 Danish 216

284 Finnish 216

Finland-Swedish 218

285 What is Finland-Swedish? 218

286 Ålandian Swedish 218

287 High Swedish – A Finnish standard 219

288 Kotus 219

289 Vowels 220

290 The *sje* and *tje* sounds 221

291 *R* 221

292 Retroflex consonants 221

293 /dj/ 221

294 Pitch accents 221

295 The quantity rule 222

296 Ease of understanding 222

297 Finland-Swedish reductions 222

298 *De/dem* 222

299 The extra *att* 222

300 *Nog* 223

301 May we use *Ni* in Finland? 223

302 The wacky *fast* 223

303 Temporal expressions 224

304 *Som bäst* 225

305 Finland-Swedish – Sweden-Swedish glossary 225

Notes & Acknowledgements 229

Sources 231

Index 234

Foreword

I can, with confidence, inform you that there is no lack of textbooks, nor grammar books, in the world. Books that the least of us would read voluntarily on a cozy Sunday evening even with unlimited whisky at our disposal. Although we really, truly want to learn a language – be it for work, to find friends, or to order an ice cold beer from a hole in the wall in a foreign country – books like that can make it feel like homework.

Fortunately, this is not a textbook, nor is it a grammar book. This is a book of epiphanies, a book of revelations, even. Imagine this being your study buddy, your personal native Swede, a collection of short sticky-note sized chunks of information. It's the book you turn to when you notice something peculiar and inexplicable, when you're demotivated and in tears, craving answers. This *lagom* handbook will care for you and keep you safe.

Why *lagom*? This world-famous Swedish word expresses that something is just right. It's a very subjective word, however it's what we use when something is good enough for us. It's not a textbook, nor is it a grammar book. It contains a mix of some basic grammar but focuses on the most common errors learners make, the most common questions they ask me, and other topics that could startle and confuse the learner. If there were a shortcut to learning a language, this would be it.

I'm not a schooled language teacher, but the passion for languages, especially my native one, has driven me to learn more, analyze, question, and ultimately teach it online. The spark that started it all was when I started to look into German material for learning Swedish. The errors and questionable statements, that I as a native speaker couldn't agree with at all, kept piling up and I decided to step up and to try and teach my native language as accurately as possible from a modern point of view.

So I started a website, that turned into a podcast, that turned into a YouTube channel, and during the last 10+ years I've helped a lot of people become fluent in Swedish. With this, I've also gained insight into the quirks of my own mother tongue, as well as the frequent mistakes beginners make. Ever since the beginning I've been wanting to publish a book and now, celebrating a decade of teaching Swedish online, the idea of what I wanted this book to be formed.

Do you know that feeling when you stumble upon a small linguistic detail that no one really teaches you and it makes you feel like you've discovered a secret that you're not supposed to know and that will help push you into fluency quicker? It's the best feeling in the world and with this book I want you to have that experience – over and over again.

This is your *lagom* guide to Swedish.

Mycket nöje! – enjoy!

How to Use This Book

This book has been written to the best of my abilities, trying to break down basic grammar as well as topics that could startle the learner and questions that often get asked over and over again. The information is not only presented to you, the reader, backed by sources but also has part of my own feel for my native language baked in. It is my intention for you to be able to learn natural contemporary Swedish as well as to get insight in older, regional, and formal Swedish to avoid as much frustration and confusion as possible.

Be advised that other speakers might feel differently about one or two things in this book because it is not how people speak in their area. My focus is, however, for you to be able to understand Swedish as spoken in the media, which is heavily influenced by Central Swedish and the Stockholm dialect(s). Largely regional traits have of course been marked as such.

Writing a book about the essence of a language is difficult without using technical terms. It's something that I've deliberately tried to steer clear of, however, in some cases, trying to write around them can end up to be more confusing. It is assumed that the reader of this book does know at least the basic parts of speech (noun, verb, adjective) but a few additional and recurring terms in this book that you as a learner and reader ought to know are the following:

perfect	The past tense, created with *to have* – *has gone*, *has looked*, *has eaten*, and *has listened*.
past perfect	The past tense, created with the past tense of *to have* – *had gone*, *had looked*, *had eaten*, and *had listened*.
present continuous	A verb form expressing ongoing actions – *is going*, *is looking*, *is eating*, and *is listening*.
supine	A dedicated verb form that exists only to create the perfect and past perfect tenses in Swedish – *har/hade gått*, *har/hade tittat*, *har/hade ätit*, and *har/hade lyssnat*.
infinitive	The basic unconjugated form of a verb – *to go*, *to look*, *to eat*, and *to listen*.
present/past participle	An adjective form sprung from a verb – *a walking girl*, *an eaten apple*.
passive voice	Used when an action is performed on something or

someone – *to be eaten*.

As opposed to the active voice where someone is actively performing the action – *to eat*.

prefix	A letter combination attached to the front of a word.
suffix	The opposite of a prefix. A few letters attached to the end of the word to modify it.
conjugate	To modify a verb according to tense, voice, mood, etc.
decline	To modify a noun or adjective into the desired form according to definitiness, number, gender, etc.
compare	To modify an adjective according to the desired degree of comparison – *easy*, *easier*, *easiest*.
voiced	A sound made **with** the the vocal cords (e.g. /b/, /d/, /g/).
voiceless	A sound made **without** the vocal cords (e.g. /p/, /t/, /k/).

deponent verbs	Swedish verbs that end on an *-s* and look like verbs in the passive voice.

Furthermore, different ways of visualizing pronunciation are used throughout this book.

1. When square brackets are used, the pronunciation is written with the standard phonetic alphabet as accurate as it needs to be for the context.

välkommen [vɛːlkɔmːən] – welcome

2. When slashes are used, **the regular Swedish alphabet** is used. Long sounds are symbolized by four letters. In consonant combinations with only one sound, every letter is doubled. Where stress is important for the explanation, stressed syllables are written in capital letters and separated from the rest with a dash for legibility.

välkommen /VÄÄÄÄL-KOMMMM-en/ – welcome

3. To help identify particle verbs, with stress on the particle, those have been underlined.

Jag <u>hälsar på</u>. – I'm visiting.

 For a more immersive experience, you can download the audio of all the examples in this book for free at:
https://www.sayitinswedish.com/books/a-lagom-guide-to-swedish/

The Basics

1   Swedish is a Germanic language which ultimately belongs to the Indo-European language family. Nouns in some of these languages have two forms:

1. The **indefinite** form, which is recognized by the lack of article or by adding *a* or *an* to the word in English, *ein* or *eine* in German, *een* in Dutch, *un* and *une* in French, *uno* and *una* in Spanish, etc.
▷ **3, the Swedish indefinite form**

2. The **definite** form, which is constructed by putting the article *the* in front of the noun in English, *der*, *die*, or *das* in German, *de* and *het* in Dutch, *le* and *la* in French, *el* and *la* in Spanish, and so on.
▷ **4, the Swedish definite form**

2   Where German has three so-called grammatical genders, Dutch, French, and Spanish have two, the Swedish nouns also have two grammatical genders: *utrum* (the common gender) and *neutrum* (the neuter gender). For the sake of simplicity, this book will continue to refer to them as *en* words and *ett* words according to their corresponding indefinite articles.

3   **The indefinite form in Swedish** is constructed by adding

the article *en* or *ett,* depending on the gender, in front of the noun. These are equivalent to English *a/an.*

en bil – a car

ett hus – a house

4   **The definite form in Swedish** is achieved by adding a suffix to the noun instead of an article. The endings are generally *-(e)n* for *en* words and *-(e)t* for *ett* words. This is equivalent to the English article *the.*

bilen – the car

huset – the house

5   When adding adjectives into the mix, Swedish utilizes a so-called double definite form, adding an additional article in front of the adjective beside the noun's definite suffix. These are *den* for *en* words and *det* for *ett* words.
▷ **42, adjectives**

den stora bilen – the big car

det stora huset – the big house

These can also be used as demonstrative pronouns equivalent to English *that.*
▷ **61, demonstrative pronouns**

den bilen – that car

det huset – that house

6 There are several ways to construct the plural of a Swedish noun, which can end up being quite tricky business.

The noun will take one of five or six endings (depending on which grammatician you're asking) but there is generally no solid way to know what the plural of a noun is and I recommend that you just learn the plural together with the singular form as you go instead of wasting time with every single exception.

There are tons of little rules and exceptions which are beyond the scope of this book. This is not trying to be a grammar book, remember?

7 Roughly and in short, we can say that *en* words ending on an -*a* switch that out for the ending -*or*. Some nouns that end on an -*e* also belong to this group.

en flicka, två flickor – a girl, two girls

en ände, två ändar – an end, two ends

8 *En* words ending on a consonant usually get the plural suffix -*ar*. This also goes for some words ending on an -*e* and one syllable words ending on a long vowel.

en skog, två skogar – a forest, two forests

en tomte, två tomtar – a gnome/Santa Claus, two gnomes/Santa Clauses

en sjö, två sjöar – a lake, two lakes

9 Sometimes nouns ending on a consonant will get the ending -*er* added instead.

en röst, två röster – a voice/vote, two voices/votes

10 Swedish nouns ending on -*e* or sometimes another vowel get the ending -*r* slapped on.

en fiende, två fiender – an enemy, two enemies

en sko, två skor – a shoe, two shoes

11 Finally, if the noun ends on -*er* or -*are*, there is no plural suffix at all.

en lärare, två lärare – a teacher, two teachers

Some other words utilize a vowel change instead of a plural ending (and some both).

en man, två män – a man, two men

12 Which plural ending an *ett* word gets is, on the other hand, a bit easier to guess.

Ett words ending on a vowel get the plural suffix -*n* and those ending on a consonant get nothing added to them. Thus the singular and the plural both look identical. There is no way around this, I'm sorry.

ett äpple, två äpplen – an apple, two apples

ett barn, två barn – a child, two children

13 When you've nailed the indefinite plural form of a noun, the definite plural should be a piece of cake.

They all end on *-na* **except** *ett* words ending on a consonant, which get the suffix *-en* added. The plural suffix *-n* only gets an *-a*, since there is already an *-n* present.

Here is a list with the plural suffixes and their corresponding definite endings:

-or	-na	*en* words
-ar	-na	*en* words
-er	-na	*en* words
-r	-na	*en* words
-n	-a	*ett* words
-	-en	mostly *ett* words

There are a few exceptions, like *öga* (eye) and *öra* (ear), which turn into *ögon* (eyes) and *öron* (ears) in plural.

14 Uncountable nouns don't take an article, just like in English. These can be words like liquids, abstract concepts or other things that don't lose their properties when divided. A bit of milk is still going to be milk, whereas a piece of a stove is not a stove.

Jag dricker mjölk. – I drink milk.

15   Despite this, even countable items can be used in an uncountable manner when defining a type of something.

Det luktar fisk. – It smells like fish.

16   When talking about something in general, Swedish makes use of so-called naked nouns. This means that these words are, similarly to the uncountable nouns, used without an article.

Jag har bil. – I've got a car.
(Focus is on the speaker's ability to provide a car or to add his expertise about owning a car to the conversation.)

Jag har en bil. – I've got a car.
(Focus is on the speaker's car.)

17   The possessive form is expressed with the ending *-s*. Beware of the missing apostrophe in Swedish.

kattens tassar – the cat's paws

bilens däck – the car's tires

18   Sometimes we use prepositions to talk about the features of something instead of using the *-s* suffix.

taket på huset – the roof of (on) the house

husets tak – the roof of the house

19   Compounds in Swedish are constructed by fusing words together into one long word, something that often startles and even scares the native English speaker who is used to separating the words with spaces or breaking the words up with the preposition *of*.

tåg (train) + station (station) = tågstation (train station)

efter (after) + rätt (dish) = efterrätt (dessert)

Remember, that the main meaning is that of the last noun in the compound. A *tågstation* thus is primarily a station, not a train, and the *efterrätt* is a dish.

Words often lose their ending vowel and/or get a connector of some sort like *-e*, *-s*, *-o*, or *-a*[1]. This is however quite inconsistent, but good to know when you see a compound. Generally speaking, though, a word that already is a compound is fused together with others with an *-s-*.

tågstationsbyggnad – train station building

Longer words are theoretically possible, nothing is stopping you, but are obviously avoided, since the length limits legibility.

Be aware that there is no such thing as a triple consonant in Swedish, which can get confusing for a learner when some compounds end up looking the same. This is rarely a problem in real life.

---

[1] These often go hand in hand with old possessive forms and aren't used with new compounds or even established ones: *kyrkogård* (cemetery) but *kyrktorn* (church tower).

glasskål (glas + skål) – glass bowl

glasskål (glass + skål) – ice cream bowl

glasskål (glass + kål) – ice cream cabbage

20 Swedish verbs are, compared to many other languages, very straightforward. They are conjugated only with time and mood in mind and never person or number. There are, however, four groups to consider, making things a little bit trickier. We call these conjugation groups.

The first conjugation group contains most verbs, since it's also the only one where new verbs end up. Consider the verb *swisha* which is a new word with the meaning *to transfer money with the Swedish mobile payment app Swish*.

▷ **243, create your own verbs**

Infinitive	Present	Past	Supine
swisha	swishar	swishade	swishat

21 The second conjugation group is similar to the first one with the difference that the infinitive ending -*a* doesn't attach to the stem and, thus, is absent throughout the conjugation table.

Worth noting is also that the past tense ending -*de* turns into a -*te* depending on the stems ending consonant being voiced (-*de*) or voiceless (-*te*).

▷ **104, assimilation**

If the stem already ends on a -d or -t, and the vowel is short, only an -e is added to it. If it is long, the vowel gets shortened in spoken Swedish, marked by a double (and thus pronounced long) consonant.

▷ 89, the quantity rule

Verb stems on -r generally don't get any extra suffix in the present tense.

Infinitive	Present	Past	Supine
höra (to hear)	hör	hörde	hört
läsa (to read)	läser	läste	läst
föda (to give birth)	föder	födde	fött
mäta (to measure)	mäter	mätte	mätt

22   The third conjugation group looks similar to the second group but contains only a handful of single syllable words with a long vowel that gets shortened in the past tense.

Infinitive	Present	Past	Supine
må (to feel)	mår	mådde	mått
bo (to live)	bor	bodde	bott

sy (to sew)	syr	sydde	sytt
fly (to flee)	flyr	flydde	flytt

23   The fourth conjugation group is all about strong verbs. This means that the stem's vowel changes according to a pattern. These are sometimes mistaken for irregular verbs, although their patterns are quite regular.

It's noteworthy that there are verbs in other groups that get a vowel change as well, but otherwise follow the designated pattern of that group.

All the different patterns are outside the scope of this book. Still not a grammar book, people. But here are some common verbs:

Infinitive	Present	Past	Supine
äta (to eat)	äter	åt	ätit
sjunga (to sing)	sjunger	sjöng	sjungit
gråta (to cry)	gråter	grät	gråtit
bli (to become)	blir	blev	blivit
dricka (to drink)	dricker	drack	druckit

| flyga (to fly) | flyger | flög | flugit |

Worth noting is that, since they construct the supine form with the ending *-it*, also words that **don't** change their vowel belong to this group. This is indeed a confusing group.

Infinitive	Present	Past	Supine
sova (to sleep)	sover	sov	sovit

24   Swedish also has genuine irregular verbs that don't follow any of the patterns discussed so far.

Infinitive	Present	Past	Supine
vilja (to want)	vill	ville	velat
skola (will)	ska	skulle	skolat
kunna (can)	kan	kunde	kunnat
veta (to know)	vet	visste	vetat

25   Just as in English, the past tense is constructed with the past tense form of the verb.

This tense is used for story telling, when the time is known, or the action has been completed[2].

Jag jobbade i går. – I worked yesterday.

Jag snubblade. – I tripped.

26 The perfect tense is also used for talking about the past. It is constructed by the helper verb *ha* (to have) and the verb's supine form. This form is only used for constructing the perfect and past perfect tense.

▷ **39, helper verbs**

This tense is used for expressing that something in the past still has relevance in the present. It expresses actions that were initiated in the past and aren't completed[3] or are at least still true, like experiences that once were made, or actions that happened recently, so that they are considered current.

Jag har varit i Sverige. – I've been to Sweden.
(The experience has been made.)

Han har bott här i fem år. – He has been living here for five years.
(He's still living there.)

Du har tappat dina nycklar. – You've lost your keys.
(They are still not in your possession.)

---

[2] In the past, this tense has been called *imperfekt* but since it indicates that the action has been completed, the terminology has been changed to *preteritum* in contemporary Swedish grammar.

[3] In other languages, the perfect tense is used when an action has ended (as opposed to imperfect).

Jag har jobbat i dag. – I've been working today.
(Both the regular past tense and the perfect tense work here, since today can be a point in the past but is at the same time within the scope of the present.)

27   The past perfect is used with the same conditions as perfect but the focus is on the past and not the present. It thus expresses that something happened even further back in the past.

När gästerna kom hade han väntat i 2 timmar. – When the guests arrived, he had waited for 2 hours.

Before the past	Past
han hade väntat	när gästerna kom
he had waited	when the guests arrived

28   The future tense can be expressed in several ways, either with the present tense, or commonly with one of the following helper verbs: *skola*, *komma (att)*, and *tänka*.

In Swedish, the future action is implied when the present tense is accompanied by an adverbial that indicates a point in time or from the context.

Jag går till skolan imorgon. – I'm going to go to school tomorrow.

Det blir regn. – We're getting rain.

29   When the intent of a future action is particularly strong, the present tense of *skola* is used: *ska*[4].

Jag ska gå till skolan imorgon. – I will be going to school tomorrow.

30 The use of *komma (att)* indicates that a prediction has been made.

Det kommer att regna imorgon. – It will rain tomorrow.

It is very common to leave out *att* (to) in this case.
▷ **39, helper verbs**

31 If the speaker has a loose intent of doing something, the verb *tänka* (to think) is used.

Jag tänker gå till skolan imorgon. – I am going to go to school tomorrow.
(But something might come up.)

32 Some verbs can't stand alone without a reflexive pronoun as their object. These are called reflexive verbs.
▷ **59, reflexive pronouns**

Paret gifter sig. – The couple is getting married.

Jag betedde mig illa. – I behaved badly.

33 A bunch of regular verbs can also act as reflexive verbs, when

---

[4] An alternative older spelling of *ska* is *skall*, which is important to know, but the variant has gotten the boot and is on its way out the door. Personally, I stopped using it some 10 years ago.

the object is the same as the subject.

Du kan skada dig! – You could get hurt!
(lit. "You could hurt you.")

but

De skadade en polis. – They hurt a police officer.

34 The passive voice is constructed either by adding the suffix *-s* to the verb or using the verbs *bli* or *vara* + the past participle of the main verb. The so-called agent, the one performing the action, is marked with the preposition *av* (by), when present.
▷ **49, participle**

Katten jagas av hunden. – The cat is chased by the dog.

Katten blir jagad av hunden. – The cat is getting chased by the dog.

Katten är jagad av hunden. – The cat is being chased by the dog.

35 Unfortunately, there are also verbs that look like they are in the passive voice because they always end on an *-s*. They aren't.

These are called deponent verbs. Confusing, yes.

Let's divide these into three groups, to get to know these types of verbs a bit better. One of these contains the genuine deponents that don't exist in any other form.

Infinitive	Present	Past	Supine
andas (to breathe)	andas	andades	andats
lyckas (to succeed)	lyckas	lyckades	lyckats
låtsas (to pretend)	låtsas	låtsades	låtsas
trivas (to like it)	trivs	trivdes	trivts

▷ 218, *trivas*

36 Then there are the ones that I'd like to call the "false passives", since they basically look like they could be the passive form of another verb but in reality have an entirely different meaning. I'm sorry.

Infinitive	Present	Past	Supine
hoppas (to hope)	hoppas	hoppades	hoppats
hoppa (to jump)	hoppar	hoppade	hoppat
fattas (to be missing)	fattas	fattades	fattats
fatta (to grasp)	fattar	fattade	fattat

37 Regular verbs in the active voice can also form deponent verbs, when two parties are the common denominator in an action, equivalent to using *varandra* (each other), or when the state, that the action expresses, is ongoing or often occurs.

Swedish doesn't have a present continuous tense to express an ongoing action, but this construction would be one of the ways to kind of express this tense.

Infinitive	Present	Past	Supine
träffas (to be meeting)	träffas	träffades	träffats
träffa (to meet)	träffar	träffade	träffat

Vi träffade varandra på internet. – We met each other on the internet.

Vi träffades på internet. – We met (each other) on the internet.

Pojkarna slåss. – The boys are fighting (each other).

De pussas. – They're kissing (each other).

Han slåss. – He (usually) starts a fight/is fighting.

Hon nyps. – She (usually) pinches/is pinching.

Det bränns. – It burns.

(The burning state is ongoing.)

38   Compounds made up of a verb and an adverb or preposition are called particle verbs, which can have totally different meanings than the counterpart without a particle.

Infinitive	Present	Past	Supine
hälsa (to greet)	hälsar	hälsade	hälsat
hälsa på[5] (to visit)	hälsar på	hälsade på	hälsat på

Some particle verbs also have a variant where the particle is a prefix. This often means that the meaning is a bit more abstract.

Jag <u>bryter av</u> grenen. – I'm breaking the branch.

Avbryt mig inte! – Don't interrupt me!

In the participle, the particle is always a prefix.

en avbruten gren – a snapped branch

ett avbrutet möte – an interrupted meeting

Examples of how different the meanings of particle verbs can

---

[5] Particle verbs have the stress on their particles. This can be confusing to learners when *hälsa* (to greet) takes an object and needs the preposition *på*, making it look identical to *hälsa på* (to visit), with the stress, however, occurring on the verb.

be:

komma	to come
komma ihåg	to remember
komma på	to think of
komma fram	to come to the conclusion
komma över	to get over
komma undan	to get away

As you can see, these kinds of verbs also exist in English.

39 Helper verbs are conjugated verbs that come together with a main verb in the infinitive. These can be divided roughly into three groups:

1. Traditional helper verbs that don't need the infinitive marker *att* (to) in front of the infinite verb.

Infinitive	Present	Past	Supine
(skola) (will)	ska	skulle	(skolat)
(böra) (should)	bör	borde	(bort)
(måsta) (to have to)	måste	måste	(måst)

kunna (can)	kan	kunde	kunnat
behöva (to need)	behöver	behövde	behövt
vilja (to want)	vill	ville	velat
få (to be allowed to)	får	fick	fått

Jag måste gå. – I have to go.

Jag ska göra det. – I will do that.

Jag behöver gå till affären. – I need to go to the store.

Han vill träffa dig. – He wants to meet you.

2. Verbs that often act like helper verbs and mostly get *att* omitted because of this.

Infinitive	Present	Past	Supine
komma (to come)	kommer	kom	kommit
hinna (to make it in time)	hinner	hann	hunnit
börja (to begin)	börjar	började	börjat

orka (to have enough energy)	orkar	orkade	orkat
slippa (to not have to do, to be excused from)	slipper	slapp	sluppit
försöka (to try)	försöker	försökte	försökt
hjälpa (to help)	hjälper	hjälpte	hjälpt
glömma (to forget)	glömmer	glömde	glömt

Jag kommer (att) resa bort. – I'm going to go away.

Vi hinner inte (att) sova. – We don't have time to sleep.

Hon börjar (att) äta utan dig. – She's going to start eating without you.

Kvinnan orkar (att) springa. – The woman has the energy to run.

Du slipper (att) städa. – You don't have to clean.

Barnet försöker (att) simma. – The child tries to swim.

Vi hjälper dig (att) städa. – We'll help you clean.

3. Regular verbs that sporadically stand in front of other verbs and aren't really helper verbs and are also not seen as such by the speaker and thus **need** the infinitive marker *att*.

Han väljer att stanna. – He chooses to stay.

Jag <u>ser fram</u> emot att resa. – I look forward to travel.

40   The subjunctive mood[6] is used to express possible or non-real events, wishes, hopes, and opinions.

In modern Swedish, there is barely any dedicated verb form left that expresses this mood and therefore the past tense or helper verbs are used instead.

▷ **161, personal verb conjugations**

The present subjunctive mood expresses wishes and hopes and is constructed with the helper verb *må* (may).

Må du lyckas i livet. – May you be successful in life.

41   The past subjunctive mood is constructed with the past tense or with the helper verb *skulle* (the past tense of *skola*). In English, the mood can be recognized with a little help from conditional helper verbs (he.he.) like *would* or *should*, or an if clause.

---

[6] In Swedish, the subjunctive mood has merged with the optative mood, which expresses wishes and hopes, and the conditional mood, which expresses conditions.

Det skulle vara bra. – It would be good.

Om jag fick en leksak. – If I got a toy.

42 Adjectives need to change depending on grammatical gender and number. This means that they look slightly different for *en* words, *ett* words, and words in plural.

en stor bil – a big car

ett stort hus – a big house

stora bilar – big cars

stora hus – big houses

If the adjective ends on -*ad*, the plural form is expressed with an -*e* instead of an -*a*.

en skadad hund – a hurt dog

två skadade hundar – two hurt dogs

43 Two things are noteworthy here: the plural form also serves as the definite form of an adjective (watch out for the double definite) and the *ett* variant is also used as an adverb (similar to how English adjectives can be turned into adverbs with the suffix -*ly*).

▷ **5, the double definite**

den stora bilen – the big car

det stora huset – the big house

den skadade hunden – the injured dog

en snabb bil – a fast car

Bilen åker snabbt. – The car goes fast.

The definite form of the adjective is also used after possessive pronouns.

min stora bil – my big car

44 Most Swedish adjectives are compared with the endings *-are* and *-ast*. A handful get the ending *-re* and *-st* instead.

First degree	Second degree	Third degree
snabb (fast)	snabbare (faster)	snabbast (fastest)
hög (high)	högre (higher)	högst (highest)

To compare things in a sentence, you use *än* (than).

Din bil är snabbare än min. – Your car is faster than mine.

45 Adjectives can also be compared with the words *mer* (more) and *mest* (most). Words ending on *-ad*, *-ande*, *-ende*, and *-isk* tend to take this pattern.

mer/mest road – more/most amused

mer/mest levande – more/most living

mer/mest leende – more/most smiling

mer/mest fantastisk – more/most fantastic

This way of comparing can theoretically be used with any adjective and is indeed sometimes used alongside comparison with suffixes. One way is just more common with some words, less used with others.

A rule of thumb is to use this pattern with words that would get too long and bulky otherwise and to be observant: with which words do native Swedes use which pattern?

46   There are also a few adjectives like *bra* (good), *dålig* (bad), *liten* (small), and *gammal* (old) with irregular forms.

First degree	Second degree	Third degree
bra (good)	bättre	bäst
dålig (bad)	sämre	sämst
liten (small)	mindre	minst
gammal (old)	äldre	äldst

47   Like the first degree, the **third degree** has to change in the definite form.

den snabbaste bilen – the fastest car

de snabbaste bilarna – the fastest cars

In addition, as you can see in the example, the definite form of the third degree gets the ending *-e* as opposed to *-a*.

48 Some adjectives aren't declined according to grammatical gender and number and are thus compared with *mer/mest* since they don't receive any endings. A good rule of thumb is to look at the ending. If the adjective ends on an unstressed vowel, the suffix *-ande*, *-ende*, or *-s*, it will most likely look the same in all cases.

en lila jacka – a purple jacket

två lila jackor – two purple jackets

mer/mest lila – more/most purple

49 There is one type of adjective that we haven't talked about yet and that's the so-called participle. These are special forms of a verb that are used like adjectives. These can be divided into two groups: the present participle and the past participle.

The present participle can't be modified and describes a feature of a noun based on what it is doing in the present. It's constructed with the verb's stem and the suffix *-ande* or, when the verb ends on a long vowel, *-ende*.

Infinitive	Present	Present participle
baka (to bake)	bakar	bakande
läsa (to read)	läser	läsande
sy (to sew)	syr	syende
äta (to eat)	äter	ätande

50 The past participle describes the feature or state of a noun based on what has happened in the past. It is constructed from the supine form of the verb and changes like a regular adjective.

▷ 42, adjectives

Infinitive	Supine	Past participle
baka (to bake)	bakat	bakad, bakat, bakade
läsa (to read)	läst	läst, läst, lästa
sy (to sew)	sytt	sydd, sytt, sydda
äta (to eat)	ätit	äten, ätet, ätna

The sharp-eyed reader has already noticed that when the stem ends on a voiceless consonant, the expected -*d* turns into -t in the past participle causing both the *en* word and *ett* word forms to look the same.

▷ 104, assimilation

The second thing worth noting is that the verbs of the fourth conjugation group end on -*it* in supine but -*en* in the participle.

▷ 23, the fourth conjugation group

51 Adverbs generally describe how something is done but could also be any other word describing time, way, space, degree, etc. Question words also belong to this part of speech as well as negations.

The most basic adverb, or in contemporary Swedish grammar an adverbial adjective, is sprung from the *ett* word variant of an adjective and is also compared in the same way.

▷ **42, adjectives**

Bilen åker snabbt. – The car goes fast.

Han hoppar högt. – He jumps high.

52   Some adverbs come in both a form that expresses a location and one that expresses a direction.

Direction	Location
hem (home)	hemma (at home)
bort (away)	borta (gone)
upp (up -wards)	uppe (up)
ner[7] (down -wards)	nere (down)
in (in)	inne (inside)
ut (out)	ute (outside)
fram (forwards)	framme[8] (at the front)

---

[7] This word is also spelled *ned*. Both spellings are just as accepted but *ned* is the only choice in some compounds. *Ner* is more common but not really used in formal situations.

[8] *Fram/Framme* are also used in the context of a trip and are the equivalent to

hit (here, hither)	här (here)
dit (there, thither)	där (there)

53 Since this isn't a grammar book (told you) we're not going to talk much more about adverbs and adverbials specifically. But since this is a handbook, I'm going to provide you with a list with a bunch of useful adverbs.

nu	now
då	then
snart	soon
nyss	just now, recently
alltid	always
ofta	often
ibland	sometimes
igen	again
redan	already
aldrig	never
när som helst[9]	any time

English *there* in that case: *När är vi framme?* (When are we there?)/*När vi kommer fram* (When we're there).

[9] Adverbs and adverbials can also consist of several words. Important examples for

så	so
hur som helst	anyway
hur ... som helst	no matter how ..., incredibly
annorlunda	different
överallt	everywhere
någonstans	somewhere
ingenstans	nowhere
alldeles	completely
ganska	fairly, pretty, quite
nästan	almost
bara	only
ju ... desto ...	the ... the ...
också	also
heller	neither
både ... och ...	both ... and ...
alltså	so, therefore

this are indications of time like *i dag* (today), *i går* (yesterday), *förra veckan* (last week) or *nästa år* (next year).

åtminstone	at least
inte	not
gärna	gladly
tyvärr	unfortunately

54 And here are some of the most important question words or interrogative adverbs in fancy pants language.

vad?	what?
varför?	why?
var?	where?
vart?	where to?
hur?	how?
när?	when?
varifrån?[10]	where from?

55 Prepositions are words that express a relationship between two words or phrases and can often be seen as a replacement for grammatical cases in a bunch of languages.

The most basic use is that of explaining where something is

---

[10] *Varifrån* can also be divided into *var ... ifrån*: *Var kommer du ifrån?/Varifrån kommer du?* (Where are you from?).

located, the direction in which something is moving, a point in time or duration, the means with (or without) something is done, etc.

Boken ligger **på** bordet. – The book is **on** the table.

En fågel sitter **i** trädet. – A bird is sitting **in** the tree.

Vi går **till** affären. – We're walking **to** the store.

Jag stod här **före** dig. – I was standing here **before** you.

Hon stannar **i** tre veckor. – She's staying **for** three weeks.

Han slog honom **med** hammaren. – He hit him **with** the hammer.

Han lever ett liv **utan** köttbullar. – He's leading a life **without** meatballs.

56   Here is a list of prepositions that could be good to know in the beginning.

på	on
vid	at, by
bredvid	beside
under	under, during
i	in (inside)
genom	through

till	to
åt	towards
för	for
med	with
utan	without
framför	in front of
bakom	behind
mellan	between
runt	around
om	about, in (time), during
före	before
innan	before
efter	after
från och med	as of
till och med	until (time)
tills	until
tack vare	thanks to
för ... skull	for ... sake

i stället för   instead of

57   Pronouns act as substitution for a noun or nominal phrase.
When learning a language, the so-called personal pronouns
are among the first words you learn.

jag	I	mig	me
du	you	dig	you
han	he	honom	him
hon	she	henne	her
det	it	det	it
vi	we	oss	us
ni	you (plural)	er	you (plural)
de	they	dem	them

▷ **107, dom**

There are also the general pronoun *man* and the somewhat
new and less frequently used gender neutral *hen*[11], equivalent
to the singular *they* in English.

---

[11] The pronoun was first attested in 1966 but has started to gain popularity in recent
years. For some people it can feel politically loaded and it's also less likely to appear
in formal texts since it's not traditional Swedish. You can however spot it in news
articles from time to time.

man	one, you	en[12]	one, you
hen	they	hen	them

Man bör ha kläder på sig. – One should wear clothes.

Hen är lärare. – They are a teacher.

58   When expressing possession, we make use of – drumroll – possessive pronouns.

min, mitt, mina	my, mine
din, ditt, dina	your, yours
hans	his
hennes	hers
dess, dens	its
vår, vårt, våra	our, ours
er, ert, era	your, yours (plural)
deras	theirs

Where there are three forms of the same pronoun, they are selected depending on, I think you guessed it, the grammatical gender, number, and if the noun is in the definite form.

min bil – my car

---

[12] *En* is considered causal, sometimes also used as a subject, replacing *man*.

mitt hus – my house

mina katter – my cats

Dens is **only** used with people and **always** stressed, often followed by a relative subordinate clause. Where *dens* is typically used, *hens* is starting to gain some room.

Vi hjälper bara dens katt som har bett om det. – We will only help the cat of the one who has asked for it.

59 Reflexive pronouns point back to the subject of a sentence and correspond to English pronouns with the suffix *-self/-selves*. In Swedish, the personal object pronouns double as reflexive pronouns except for the third person (*he, she, they,* etc.) that share the word *sig*.

Jag tvättar mig. – I'm washing myself.

Han tvättar sig. – He's washing himself.

Han tvättar honom. – He's washing him.
(He's washing another person.)

Hon slog sig. – She got hurt.

Hon slog henne. – She punched her.

De bet sig. – They bit themselves.

De bet dem. – They bit them.

60 Following up on this, Swedish also has reflexive **possessive** pronouns for when the subject is the owner of the object. These are *sin, sitt, sina*.

▷ **58, possessive pronouns**

Hon tvättar sin bil. – She's washing her (own) car.

Hon tvättar hennes bil. – She's washing her car.
(Someone else's car.)

Han kysste sin fru. – He kissed his (own) wife.

Han kysste hans fru. – He kissed his wife.
(Some other guy's wife.)

De tittade på sina händer. – They looked at their (own) hands.

De tittade på deras händer. – They looked at their hands.

61 Demonstrative pronouns are used to directly point to and draw attention to something. They need to be declined according to grammatical gender and number. In Swedish, we can divide these into three different groups.

1. The standard *denna/detta/dessa*[13] (this/these) are followed by the indefinite form of a noun.

denna bil – this car

---

[13] In southern and western dialects, this is also used in casual settings, but together with the **definite form** of the noun.

detta hus – this house

dessa barn – these children

2. *Den/det/de här* (this/these) and *den/det/de där* (that/those) are used in spoken Swedish and in casual writing. This is the one you'll come across the most.

den här bilen – this car

den där bilen – that car

det här huset – this house

det där huset – that house

de här barnen – these children

de där barnen – those children

3. The double definite articles *den/det/de* can also be used demonstratively. They are then emphasized.

den bilen – that car

det huset – that house

de barnen – those children

62 Besides these key groups of pronouns, there are a bunch that are outside the scope of this book (not a grammar book, remember?). But here are a bunch of important ones to know.

mycket	much
många	many
lite	little
få	few
någon	someone
något	something
någonting	something
någon/något/några[14]	some
varje	every
ingen	no, none
inget	nothing
ingenting	nothing
vem	who
vilken/vilket/vilka	which
varandra	each other
vad	what
varenda/vartenda[15]	every single

---

[14] I think you can guess by now how to use these different forms.

[15] This word is about to lose its *ett* word variant.

samma	same
själv/självt/själva	self
annan/annat/andra	another
sådan/sådant/sådana	such
första	first
sista	last
likadan/likadant/likadana	same, similar
nästa	next
förra	previous
egen/eget/egna	(one's) own

63 Conjunctions and subjunctions connect sentences and are among the most important words to learn if you want to start making longer sentences that flow naturally. Compare the following examples:

Jag heter Svea. Jag kommer från Uppsala. Jag bor i Berlin.
Jag heter Svea och kommer från Uppsala men bor i Berlin.

The conjunctions make it possible to join **main clauses** together. Just learn them. They are great.

och	and

samt[16]	as well as
men	but
för	therefore
så	so, therefore

64 Subjunctions initiate **subordinate clauses** and one of the most important ones to know right off the bat is *som*, since it can be used in so many different ways and translates into many different words in English: *who, that, which, as, like, how*, etc.

Bilen som är röd. – The car that is red.

Barnet som är trött. – The child who is tired.

Du ser ut som jag. – You look like me.

Som man bäddar får man ligga. – As you make your bed so you must lie in it.[17]

Hon jobbar som pianist. – She works as a pianist.

Som du ser ut! – Look at you![18]
(lit. "as you're looking")

---

[16] *Samt* is often used to avoid repetition of *och*.

[17] The saying is equivalent to "As you sow, so shall you reap."

[18] Used negatively when the speaker is displeased with someone's looks (dirty, raggedy, etc.).

Other important subjunctions every beginner should know are:

▷ **225, *eftersom***

eftersom	because
därför att	because
för att	because
fast	although
även om	although
så att	so that
medan	while
tills	until
till dess (att)	until
än	than
genom att	by

65   Numbers in Swedish are as straightforward as in English: when you need to combine them, you just do.

tre tusen ett hundra tjugotvå – three thousand one hundred twenty two

But let's not get ahead of ourselves. Here are the words:

en/ett	one	sjutton	seventeen
två	two	arton	eighteen
tre	three	nitton	nineteen
fyra	four	tjugo	twenty
fem	five	trettio	thirty
sex	six	fyrtio	fourty
sju	seven	femtio	fifty
åtta	eight	sextio	sixty
nio	nine	sjuttio	seventy
tio	ten	åttio	eighty
elva	eleven	nittio	ninety
tolv	twelve	hundra	hundred
tretton	thirteen	tusen	thousand
fjorton	fourteen	miljon	million
femton	fifteen	miljard	billion
sexton	sixteen	biljon	trillion

One (1) can be both *ett* or *en* because of the grammatical genders. It doesn't matter which one you pick as a stand-alone number. **A huge discrepancy is the word *biljon* which** means *trillion* and not *billion*, which is *miljard* (!).

The tricky part about Swedish numbers is how we pronounce them.

▷ **111, the pronunciation of numbers**

66   Ordinal numbers are as always a little bit different.

första	first	sjuttonde	seventeenth
andra	second	artonde	eighteenth
tredje	third	nittonde	nineteenth
fjärde	fourth	tjugonde	twentieth
femte	fifth	trettionde	thirtieth
sjätte	sixth	fyrtionde	fortieth
sjunde	seventh	femtionde	fiftieth
åttonde	eighth	sextionde	sixtieth
nionde	ninth	sjuttionde	seventieth
tionde	tenth	åttionde	eightieth
elfte	eleventh	nittionde	ninetieth
tolfte	twelfth	hundrade	hundredth
trettonde	thirteenth	tusende	thousandth
fjortonde	fourteenth	miljonte	millionth

femtonde	fifteenth	miljarte	billionth
sextonde	sixteenth	biljonte	trillionth

Andra doesn't just mean *second* but also *other*. *Miljarte* is so uncommon that it barely exists. It's not to be found in any glossary and its spelling varies.

Pronunciation Secrets

67   Despite what lots of native Swedes will tell you, *rikssvenska*[1] is not a term for standard Swedish pronunciation. There is none. Standard Swedish (*standardsvenska*) refers to written Swedish or spoken Swedish with no regional vocabulary (although regionally colored pronunciation is accepted). However, when learning Swedish, the pronunciation being taught is a mix between the one closest to the written language[2], the most common and widely spread regional traits (and exceptions from the written language) as well as Central Swedish pronunciation. Thus, the pronunciation you're being taught will always sound like natural Swedish and not synthetic which is sometimes the case with standards in other languages.

In this book, I will talk about the Swedish sounds that are widespread enough throughout the language's spectrum to be considered the de facto default as well as exceptions and regionalities that you are likely to frequently encounter.

68   The Swedish vowel system is fairly complicated and contains a lot of different unique sounds. The vowels are written with

---

[1] In modern linguistics, the term *standardsvenska* is used, where *rikssvenska* still lives in everyday speech. In Finland, *högsvenska* is the term used, as opposed to *rikssvenska* that only refers to Swedish spoken in Sweden.

[2] Which in turn was influenced by the aristocracy and previously also used as media pronunciation.

the following letters: *a, e, i, o, u, y, å, ä, ö*.

Those three additional letters come after *z* in the alphabet and are not to be considered variants of *a* and *o*. They have their own distinct sounds and qualities and must be seen as such.
▷ **70, the importance of *å, ä,* and *ö***

They are divided into two groups:

1. The hard vowels *a, o, u, å*

2. The soft vowels *e, i, y, ä, ö*

69 The vowels come in at least two variants. We could call them "qualities". One is used as the long vowel and one as the short one. This means that they are in fact two different vowels that only occur in a long respectively a short variant. Where other languages use the same vowel quality for both variants, Swedish (mostly) doesn't.

a [a, ɑː]	tappa [tapːa] (to drop)	apa [ɑːpa] (monkey)
o [ʊ, uː]	dom [dʊmː] (sentence)	stor [stuːr] (big)
o [ɔ, oː]	boll [bɔlː] (ball)	sova [soːva] (to sleep)
u [ɵ, ʉː]	full [fɵlː] (full)	hus [hʉːs] (house)
å [ɔ, oː]	fånge [fɔŋːə] (prisoner)	sås [soːs] (sauce)

e [ɛ, eː]	elva [ɛlːva] (eleven)	leka [leːka] (to play)
e [æ]	herre [hærːə] (gentleman)	–
i [ɪ, iː]	lista [lɪsːta] (list)	is [iːs] (ice)
y [ʏ, yː]	sylt [sʏlːt] (jam)	yla [yːla] (to howl)

Ä and *ö* however come in two qualities that both are used in the long and short variant. The second variant is used in front of an *r* or a retroflex sound.

▷ **82, retroflex consonants**

ä [ɛ, ɛː]	ägg [ɛgː] (egg)	äga [ɛːga] (to own)
ä [æ, æː]	ärr [ærː] (scar)	lärare [læːrarə] (teacher)
ö [ø, øː]	öster [øsːtər] (East)	öga [øːga] (eye)
ö [œ, œː]	förr [fœrː] (before)	höra [hœːra] (to hear)

An unstressed *e* sound turns into a neutral vowel (so-called schwa).

enkel [ɛŋːkəl] – easy

Keep in mind that *o* and *å*[3] share [oː] and [ɔ] and *e* and *ä* share

---

[3] I already know what your question is and the answer is no, you can't know

[ɛ].

70 Despite what some people think, the diacritics (the tiny signs above letters) do bear meaning and can't just be ignored. *Å, ä,* and *ö* are letters in their own right and are not just variants of *a* and *o*.

Consider the following word pairs and their different meanings:

såga (to saw)	saga (fairy tale)
låga (flame)	laga (to fix)
tåg (train)	tag (hold)
bära (to carry)	bara (only)
män (men)	man (man)
kräm (kissel)	kram (hug)
lök (onion)	lok (train engine)
möt (meet!)	mot (against)
söva (to put to sleep)	sova (to sleep)

71 A very prominent and unique sound that learners are good at spotting, is the so-called *Viby-i*. This is an especially compressed or buzzing sounding *i* sound that originally

---

beforehand which letter to choose or how to pronounce *o* and *å*.

existed in several rural dialects (and still does) but that people today mostly identify with the big city dialects of Stockholm and Gothenburg.

It started out as an upper-class marker, since these people could go on vacation to these dialect areas. They brought it home and it eventually trickled down, also, to become a part of their regional dialect.

It's important to know that **it's not required to master this sound**. It's unnecessary for learners to try and wrap their heads around this complicated pronunciation, wasting their time with one single sound that is only a colored variant of the regular pronunciation. There is also the danger of sounding obnoxious. Most native speakers realize /i/ within a spectrum where *Viby-i* is the most extreme variant.

72   There is also a compressed *y* sound that is less talked about but also works just like the *Viby-i*.
▷ 71, *Viby-i* (compressed, buzzing *i*)

73   In western Swedish (and in Norwegian) there is an additional vowel that is often written as ô, pronounced [ɞ], and that could be referenced as a vowel somewhere between /å/ and /ö/. It is mostly approximated to /ö/ by the rest of the Swedish speaking population when using classic dialect words that have spread outside their area of origin.

tjôta (to chat)
(In standard Swedish tjata means to nag.)

gôtt (nice)
(In standard Swedish gott means good or delicious.)

It is often referred to as the tenth vowel and developed in the Middle Ages from the old Swedish short *å* sound.

It's not expected nor is it required for anyone learning Swedish to master it to sound native. Its occurrence is regional and this is only to be considered a fun fact.

74 In the Stockholm area and Central Swedish, the short *ö* sound is reduced to /u/.

fönster /funnnnster/ – window

dörr /durrrr/ – door

Some people (including yours truly) only reduce [œ], that occurs in front of an *r* (and retroflex consonants).
▷ **69, vowel qualities**

dörr /durrrr/ – door
(But fönster remains /fönnnnster/.)

75 In Central Swedish, vowels are diphthongized because of the sound change that occurs when the jaw is relaxed. *Å* is then pronounced like /åe/ [oːᵊ], *ä* like /äe/ [ɛːᵊ], and *ö* like /öe/ [øːᵊ].

Some other sounds that slide between several sounds are *i* and *y* that sound like /i(j)e/ [iː(j)ᵊ] and /y(j)e/ [yː(j)ᵊ], and *u* and *o* that tend to be followed by a sound similar to the English *w*:

[ʉːᵝ] and [uːᵝ].

This is a question that turns up now and then because people have heard me speak in my audio and video lessons online and have gotten confused by the way I pronounce vowels.

This is nothing the learner needs to pay any attention to whatsoever but when having such a good ear for vowel variations, it's good to know what it means.

76 One last thing to mention about the Stockholm accent is that the genuine accent replaces the long *ä* sound with a long *e* sound. Now, not everyone speaks like this anymore but I've noticed myself that it can turn up even in my own speech **from time to time.**

These are some classic words to illustrate this:

räka /reeeeka/ – shrimp

räv /reeeev/ – fox

77 One last thing about Central Swedish (I know, I know) that isn't something the learner has to, **or maybe even should do**, but that is good to know: Long *o* sounds tend to get shortened in front of voiceless plosives (p, t, k). According to the quantity rule, the following consonant is then prolonged.
▷ **89, the quantity rule**

Expected pronunciation	Central Swedish
sopa (to sweep) [suːpa]	sopa [sʊpːa]
koka (to boil) [kuːka]	koka [kʊkːa]

78 As opposed to the rather complicated Swedish vowel system (although it's at least a huge improvement from early Old Norse, phew), the consonants are a lot more straightforward. Swedish uses the basic sounds of *b, d, f, g, h, j, k, l, m, n, p, r, s, t, v, x* which at first glance are pronounced as most people would expect them to. Keep on reading to get to all the juicy exceptions.

Before anyone asks, Swedish also has the letters *c, q, w*[4] and *z*[5] but they have the same pronunciation as *s/k, k, v* and *s*, whereas the latter three occur only in loan words, names and/or old spelling.

Furthermore, *j*[6] is always a half-vowel and never /dj/ [dʒ] as in English.

79 Furthermore, Swedish has a few sounds that don't have individual letters.

---

[4] Swedish doesn't have the English half-vowel *w*. That's why mixing up *v* and *w* is a big part of the Swenglish accent.

[5] *S* and *z* are always unvoiced and thus sound the same. There is no voiced *z* sound. *Z* is sometimes pronounced /ts/ in loan words.

[6] Another thing that is extremely prominent in "Swenglish".

ɕ (The *tje* sound; pronounced close to /sh/ in English.)

ʃ (The *sje* sound; everyone's favorite, used in the infamous word *sjuksköterska* and that is similar to a cat's hiss.)

ŋ (The *ng* sound; spelled and pronounced the same as in English except in the combination **gn** which is pronounced as /ngn/.)

80 The so-called *tje* sound is typically spelled with the letter combination *tj*. It also comes in the flavor of *kj*.
▷ **84, hard and soft *k* and *g***

tjuv [ɕʉːv] – thief

kjol [ɕuːl] – skirt

Some loan words have kept their original spelling but still have the *tje* sound.

chili [ɕiːlɪ]

kiosk [ɕɔsːk]

Another exception is the word *hyssja* (to hush) which spells the sound *ssj*. Some Italian loans use *c* and *ci*.

81 The *sje*[7] sound is typically spelled with the letter combination

---

[7] Some regions and social groups don't have this sound and use the *tje* sound in its place. This substitution is also frequently used for making an upper-class sounding accent.

sj. It can also be observed in the wild as *sk*, *skj*, *stj*.

sjuk [ɧʉːk] – sick

skylt [ɧʏlːt] – sign

skjorta [ɧʊʈːa] – shirt

stjärna [ɧæːɳa] – star

Of course, also this sound has a bunch of alternative spelling in loan words.

choklad [ɧʊˈklɑː] – chocolate

schack [ɧakː] – chess

show [ɧɔʊ] – show

pen**si**on[8] [pãˈɧuːn] – pension

pa**ssi**on [paˈɧuːn] – passion

sta**ti**on [staˈɧuːn] – station

geni [ɧɛˈniː] – genius

journalist [ɧʊɳaˈlɪsːt] – journalist

One special word is *kanske* (maybe), since the pronunciation can fluctuate between /kannnn**sj**e/ and /kannnn**tj**e/.

---

[8] Vowels in front of *n* tend to be nasalized.

82   Some additional consonants without individual letters are the so-called retroflex consonants. They arise when the *r* sound, which is usually a trill or a tap, encounters *s*, *d*, *t*, *n*, and **sometimes** *l*. The tongue then bends back, trying to meet the position of both the *r* and following consonant sound.

kors [kɔʂ:] – cross

jord [juːɖ] – earth

fart [fɑːʈ] – speed

barn [bɑːɳ] – child

pärla[9] [pæː[a] – pearl

The occurrence of [ɭ] is unreliable since it's almost indistinguishable from a regular /l/ and just seldom realized.

When several of these letters meet each other, all of them end up being retroflex.

borste [bɔʂ:ʈə] – brush

And when these letters or sounds meet in word boundaries (both compounds and phrases), they also magically turn into retroflex consonants. This however does not occur if the *r* is long.

ärtsoppa [æʈːʂɔpa] – pea soup

---

[9] Retroflex consonants will, just like *r*, turn *ä* into [æ].

barrskog [barːskuːg] – coniferous forest

ett par skor [ɛt pa ˈʂkuːr] – a pair of shoes

A few loan words are also pronounced with a retroflex sound, even though you wouldn't expect them to. This occurs especially at the end of a word.

mustasch [məˈstɑːʂ] – mustache

dusch [dɵʂː] – shower

garage [gaˈrɑːʂ] – garage

bagage [baˈgɑːʂ] – luggage

grimas [grɪˈmɑːʂ] – grimace

83 The letter *r* is tricky business in Swedish. Counting all dialects, it can be pronounced in at least five different ways. Counting just my Central Swedish/Stockholm/south of Stockholm accent, *r* can have **three different sounds!**

Many learners have trouble producing an *r* sound, thinking it has to be an exaggerated trill. Fortunately, the different sounds don't have any grammatical functions and don't change the meaning of the word.

The most standard sound (if we want to go down that path) is the tap/flap [ɾ] that is often described as the *t* sound in the American English pronunciation of *water*. When emphasized, and depending on the dialect, the flap more often becomes a trill [r], which, if you've heard Spanish, would be equivalent to double *r*.

Since most media is produced in Sweden's capital, Stockholm, you're very, very likely to hear a more degraded version of the tap that is a voiced buzzing[10] sound (but with the tongue placed further up). It's basically a tap without the flapping, making it a buzzing sound instead.

In the south of Sweden, in the Skåne area, the *r* sound is a throat sound instead [ʀ, ʁ], similar to that of French or German. In some west-central dialects, several different *r* sounds can co-exist within the same word. This phenomenon is called *götaregeln* (the Göta rule). And to wrap this up, in the *Östergötland* dialect, *r* is often realized like an English *w*.

84 The consonants *k* and *g* (as well as the combination *sk*) change their pronunciation depending on which vowel group they precede.

With a little help from the names of the groups, we can figure out which kind of sound the consonants get.
▷ **68, hard and soft vowels**

1. Hard vowels give them a hard sound.

katt [kat:] – cat

---

[10] Identified as a voiced retroflex fricative [ʐ].

gubbe [gəb:ə] – old man

skata [skɑ:ta] – magpie

2. In turn, *k* is pronounced [ɕ], *g* [j], and *sk* [ɧ], in front of – drumroll – soft vowels. This **does not** occur for *k* in front of *e* and *i*, and *g* in front of *e* in unstressed ending syllables[11].

kedja [ɕe:dja] – chain

gilla [jɪl:a] – to like

skylt [ɧʏl:t] – sign

but

boken [bu:kən] – the book

bråkig [bro:kɪ] – fussy

mage [mɑ:gə] – stomach

Of course loan words make all these rules go out the window: *kille* (guy), *kör* (choir), *getto* (ghetto), and in *människa* (human) *-sk-* has a soft pronunciation because why not.

And in other non-native words, the usage varies between regions.

kex [kɛk:s] – cracker

---

[11] Except in some dialects.

kex [ɕɛk:s]
(most prominent in southern and western Sweden)

giffel[12] [gɪf:əl]
(name of a popular brand of small buns)

giffel [jɪf:əl]

85   *G* also turns soft after *l* and *r*.

älg [ɛl:j] – moose

berg [bær:j] – mountain

And in the following words: *mig, dig, sig,* and *säga.*

86   The letter combinations *dj, gj, hj,* and *lj* are all pronounced as /j/ in the beginning of a word: *djur* (animal), *gjort* (done), *hjul* (wheel), and *ljus* (light).

87   The plosives *p, t,* and *k* are aspirated in front of a vowel in a stressed syllable. This means that a little puff of air leaves the mouth after the sound has been realized and it appears to be pronounced in a more exaggerated way. In the following examples, only the first plosives are aspirated. Try it out!

pappa [pʰap:a] – dad

titta [tʰɪt:a] – to look

---

[12] The manufacturer has publicly announced that both pronunciations are just as official. The pronunciation war among Swedes continues, however.

kaka [kʰɑːka] – cookie

88   In many Swedish dialects, there is something called *tjockt l* (thick l). It is a retroflex flap [ɽ] (for those who know fancy talk) and is considered the original Swedish *l* sound.

After the huge influence from Low German, Swedes literally started to speak Swedish with a German accent, generally losing this thick *l* sound. That's why it's now considered dialectal but still exists in many rural dialects. You'll most likely hear it at some point.

As with the "tenth vowel", it's not expected nor is it required for anyone learning Swedish to master it to sound native and this is only to be considered a fun fact.

89   Any syllable with the main stress in Swedish has to be long. In practice, this means that if the syllable contains a short vowel, the following consonant has to be long and vice versa. This is called the quantity rule.

fika /fiiiika/ – coffee break
(long vowel, short following consonant)

ficka /fikkkka/ – pocket
(short vowel, long following consonant)

90   Long consonants are usually marked by a double consonant: *pappa* (dad), *titta* (to look), *finna* (to find), *möss* (mice).

A long *k*, on the other hand, is represented by *ck* (as opposed to Swedish's other Nordic sibling languages): *ficka* (pocket), *säck* (bag), *macka* (sandwich). The only exception is *och* (and) which is spelled with *ch*.

Some letters are rarely or never doubled, although their pronunciation suggests it: *leja* (to hire), *skoj* (fun), *kaja* (jackdaw).

However, the quantity rule is so strong that people usually double these consonants in casual writing, especially if the word seldom exists in writing: *dojja* (shoe, slang), *vovve* (dog, slang), *hajja* (to understand, slang).

At the end of a word, *m* and *n* are sometimes doubled and sometimes not.

dam /daaaam/ – lady

damm /dammmm/ – dam

There is however no difference in spelling between *men* (but), with a short vowel, and *men* (injury), with a long vowel.

Consonant clusters are counted as a double consonant except if they are the result of added endings.

älska /ällllska/ – to love

but

snabbt /snappppt/ – quickly

91   Only the stressed word in a sentence has long sounds. All other words have short syllables only. In the following sentence, all individual words have a long vowel (*hur, mår,* and *du*), but in the context of a sentence, only the stressed word is actually long.

Hur mår du? /hur måååår du/ – How are you?

92   Swedish has two word accents for pronouncing words with two or more syllables. For simplicity, in this book I will refer to them as **accent I** and **accent II**.

Accent I is a regular rising and sinking accent.

Accent II[13] is a rising accent with a secondary stress occurring during the tone's descent. This musical accent is unique to Swedish and Norwegian and gives the languages their special sound.

Which word accent to choose is not that easy. Learners often exaggerate the use of accent II and put it in places where it doesn't belong. Since the when and where to use it varies between dialects, some dialects don't even have it and it occurs only in emphasized words, the safest bet is to go with accent I if you're unsure. **It just isn't that important grammatically.**

---

[13] Different dialects (including Norwegian) realize accent II differently, and the dialects in Finland lack it entirely, but this book, as is traditional, focuses mainly on the Central Swedish accent.

93   Accent II is used with the indefinite plural form of an *en* word, if the stem is one syllable: *båtar* (boats), *grisar* (pigs). This is different from the definite singular form that has **accent I**: *båten* (the boat), *grisen* (the pig).

Most verb conjugations are pronounced with this melodic accent except verbs from the second and fourth conjugation group. They take **accent I** in the present tense: *läser* (reading), *sover* (sleeping), *gråter* (crying). As opposed to the infinitive, for instance, that take **accent II**: *läsa* (to read), *sova* (to sleep), *gråta* (to cry).

There are a couple of hundred words with the same spelling in Swedish that are distinguished by their different accents. These are some of the classics:

Accent I	Accent II
anden (the duck)	anden (the genie, the spirit)
biten (the piece)	biten (bitten)
stegen (the steps)	stegen (the ladder)
buren (the cage)	buren (carried)
tomten (the property, the garden)	tomten (Santa Claus)

Compounds take a variant of accent II, where the second stress falls on the last syllable instead of directly after the main stress.

motor /MOOOO-TOR/ – motor

motorsåg /MOOOO-tor-SÅÅÅÅG/ – chainsaw

No rules without exceptions and thus, among other compounds, the days of the week are pronounced with accent I **and not** accent II: *måndag*, *tisdag*, etc.

94 One of the most difficult things for non-native speakers to learn is to understand spoken Swedish. The reason for this is the amount of reductions, contractions and elisions[14] that distinguish the spoken language from the written.

For instance, the sentence "Hur mår du" (How are you?) would most likely be pronounced as /huMÅÅÅÅru/, which to the inexperienced listener would sound like one single word.

95 Some words ending on a *-t*, *-d*, *-g*, *-j*, or *-l* drop these final sounds. This is by no means a rule and every word's pronunciation has to be individually learned. Sorry.

jag /jaaaa/ – I

stad /sta/ – city
(in city names and compounds)

med /meeee/ – with

mycket /mykkkke/ – much, very

---

[14] Elision is the linguistic term for the omission of sounds.

inget /inngge/ – nothing

vid /viiii/ – by, at

dag /daaaa/ – day

nej /nääää/ – no

till /ti/ – to

träd /trääää/ – tree

god /goooo/ – good

This also occurs generally when the ending consonant is followed by another consonant.

brandsläckare /brannnnsläkkkkare/ – fire extinguisher

96   Some two syllable words with a -*d*- or -*g*- in the middle lose this sound. If a vowel follows, it might disappear as well.

dagen /daaaan/ – the day

dagar /daaaar/ – days

sedan /sennnn/ – then, later

någon /nånnnn/ – someone

något /nåtttt/ – something

några /nååååra/ – some

morgon /morrrron/ – morning

i morgon /imorrrron, imorrrrn/ – tomorrow

ledsen /lessssen/ – sad

97 *En* words ending on *-re* (or sometimes a retroflex sound) often lose the *-e-* in the **definite** form in spoken Swedish. This will transform the final sound into a retroflex *n*.

läraren /läääärarn/ – the teacher

ekorren /ekkkkorn/ – the squirrel

dörren /dörrnn/ – the door

sommaren /sommmmarn/ – the summer

trädgården /träggggårrnn/ – the garden

karlen[15] /kaaaarn/ – the man

This also goes for *en* words already ending on an *-n* in the **indefinite** form.

munnen /munnnn/ – the mouth

98 *Ett* words ending on *-en* in the definite plural might get that suffix changed to an *-a* or *-ena* in casual spoken Swedish. Just good to know.

barnen /baaaarna/ – the children

---

[15] *Karlen* (the man) is never pronounced with an *l* sound. This means that, in practice, it ends on *-(re)n* in the definite form.

husen /huuuusena/ – the house

A good word to know – that looks like it would belong to this group of words – is *trä* (wood) which is interchangeable with *träd* (tree) in colloquial Swedish.

träna /trääääna/ – the trees

träden /trääääden/ – the trees

99   The adjective ending *-ig* basically always loses its *-g-* sound[16]. This also goes for all declensions *-igt* and *-iga*.

rolig /rooooli/ – funny

tråkig /trååååki/ – boring

blåsig /blåååååsi/ – windy

100   The adjective ending *-skt* often loses its *k* in spoken Swedish. This concerns only *ett* words and the adverbial declension.

svenskt /svennnnst/ – Swedish

fantastiskt /fantasssstist/ – fantastic

hemskt /hemmmmst/ – awful

101   A particularly interesting phenomenon is that Swedish verbs often get all their endings dropped, so that they all seem to be in the infinitive.

---

[16] Looking at the examples, I'm sure you can spot that the same thing has already happened in English, where Old English *-ig* has turned into *-y*.

Infinitive	Present	Past	Supine
jobba (to work)	jobba-	jobba-	jobba-
sova (to sleep)	sove-	sov	sovi-

To clarify (and as you can see in the table) this concerns the endings -r (present tense), -(a)de (past tense), and -(a)t and -(i)t (supine). This means that a word like *må* (to be feeling) is reduced only in the present tense.

102 Even general words ending on an -r, just like the present tense of a verb, also often lose that ending in spoken Swedish.

för /fö/ – for

var /vaaaa/ – where, was

hur /huuuu/ – how

103 Words with an initial *h-* sometimes lose it in a sentence – sometimes don't.

Du har fint hår. /du a fint HÅÅÅÅR/ – You've got beautiful hair.

104 No different from other languages, Swedish pronunciation is affected by assimilation. This means that certain sounds that meet each other are modified to be easier to pronounce.

Voiceless consonants (/p/, /t/, /k/, /f/, /s/, /h/, /tj/, /sj/) rule the world, and thus voiced[17] consonants (/b/, /d/, /g/, /v/, /m/, /n/, /ng/, /j/, /l/, /r/) have to bend the knee when they meet one.

snabbt /snappppt/ – quickly

högt /hökkkkt/ – high

105 N also assimilates to an m in front of plosives. Remember those? They were /p/, /t/, /k/, /b/, /d/, /g/.

en båt /em bååååt/ – a boat

brandbil /brammmmbiiiil/ – fire engine
▷ **95, omission of endings**

106 An interesting phenomenon is the change of initial d- to r- in unstressed pronouns and the word $då$ (then). This is something most prominent in the Stockholm area, but as touched upon earlier, most media content is produced there, so it's something unavoidable because it's used millions of times.

Kom då! /KOMMMM-rå/ – Come on!

Vad gör du? /va-GÖÖÖÖ-ru/ – What are you doing?

Har det regnat? /ha-re-RENNGGNA/ – Did it rain?

---

[17] Voiced means that the vocal cords assist in making the sound, as opposed to voiceless, where, you guessed it, they remain on their coffee break.

107 The personal pronouns *de* (they) and *dem* (them) are seldom pronounced like they are written. They have been replaced with *dom*[18] in spoken and, to some extent, written Swedish. This is by no means a new word[19], but hasn't been considered standard in modern Swedish writing. This is about to change but we're not completely there yet.

I recommend that you always use *dom* in spoken Swedish but *de/dem* in writing (especially in a professional setting).

108 *Är* (am, is, are) is almost exclusively pronounced /ee/ or /ää/.

As an added bonus, the supine form *varit* is pronounced /vart/ [vaʈ:], dropping the *-i-* from the last syllable. This makes the word go from two syllables (with accent II) to one syllable. The vowel is also shortened and *r* and *t* merged to a retroflex [ʈ].

Jag har varit i Sverige. /ja a vart i svärrrrje/ – I've been to Sweden.

109 *Och* (and) and the infinitive marker *att* (to) are both almost always pronounced /å/, confusing not only to learners but also to native Swedes.

Jag gillar att läsa. /ja jilar å lääääsa/ – I like to read.

Jag går och sover. /ja går å sååååver/ – I'm going to bed.

---

[18] In some dialects there are more variants, like /di/.

[19] Going all the way back to Old Swedish *þom*, first attested in the mid-1300s in the book "En nyttigh Bok om Konnunga Styrilse och Höfdinga".

These two constructions are sometimes confused by native speakers in writing: ~~Jag gillar och läsa~~ (~~I like and read~~).

110 It is completely natural to pronounce the plural ending *-or* the same as *-er*. This is not to be considered especially casual. The spelling of the suffix *-or* is based on the Old Swedish pronunciation[20], which originates in Old Norse, and has, due to its presence in written Swedish, regained its position in spoken Swedish.

Try to reduce that *-o-* to an [ə] for a more confident sound.

flickor /flikkkker/ – girls

kyrkor /tjyrrrrker/ – churches

tröjor /tröjjjjer/ – shirts

Some nouns will, however, sound the same in plural because of this, so always try to pay attention to the context in which a word appears.

färger /färrrrjer/ – colors

färjor /färrrrjer/ – ferries

111 Plural endings aren't the only things where an *o* turns into an *e*. In speech, the ending *-o* in *nio* (nine) and *tio* (ten) turns into *-e*.

---

[20] The Old Testament was published in Swedish for the first time in 1526, paving the way for a unified written Swedish.

In numbers greater than 10 the *-o* gets dropped completely: *trettio* /tretttti/ (30), *sextio* /sekkkksti/ (60), *nittio* /nitttti/ (90).

21–29 loses the *-go* in *tjugo*: *tjugoett* (21) /tjuetttt/, *tjugotvå* /tjutvåååå/ (22).

Fyrtio (40) is often pronounced /förrtti/ or /furrtti/, getting the /y/ reduced to /ö/, which you already know is often replaced with an *u* sound in Central Swedish.
▷ **74, when /ö/ becomes /u/**

112 The pronouns *vilken*, *vilket*, and *vilka* (which) tend to lose the *-l-*, prolonging the *-k-*.

Vilken? /vikkkken/ – Which?

Beware, that you have to choose the right one according to the grammatical gender and number as usual.

Vilken bil? /vikkkken bil/ – What car?

Vilket hus? /vikkkket hus/ – What house?

Vilka barn? /vikkkka barn/ – What children?

113 As an extra level of confusion, the *v-* in *vilken*, *vilket*, and *vilka* is sometimes pronounced /s/. What it really is, is an **informal** contraction of *se* (see!) + *vilken*, *vilket*, or *vilka*, and not used in writing.

Sicken otur! /siken ooootuuuur/ – Too bad!

Sicket väder! /siket vääääder/ – What weather!

Sicka snygga skor! /sika snyga skoooor/ – Nice shoes!

Compare the above sentences to the following:

Vilken otur! /viken ooootuuuur/ – Too bad!

Vilket väder! /viket vääääder/ – What weather!

Vilka snygga skor! /vika snyga skoooor/ – Nice shoes!

114 Some words have unexpected and/or rule-breaking pronunciations. The most prominent example is *fan* (the devil) which is also used for swearing. It has a long vowel, which however often is divided into two syllables. This causes the word to often have the wrong vowel quality ([a:] instead of [ɑ:]) and to be pronounced with the melodic accent II. It thus kind of acts as if it in reality has **two short *a* sounds in a row**. This pronunciation is common but not exclusive.

fan [faan, fa:n, fɑ:n] – the devil, damn!

If you recognize the elements in a compound word but can't wrap your head around its pronunciation, it might have become subject to lexicalization. This is just fancy speak for "we stopped seeing you as a compound, you're a real boy now, Pinocchio."

Smörgås[21] (sandwich) consists of *smör* (butter) and *gås*

---

[21] The word used to refer to the lumps of butter swimming on the surface of the

(goose), which both have long vowels. The compound, however, has gotten both vowels shortened (or only the first, depending on whom you're asking) and, according to the quantity rule, their consonants prolonged: /smörrrrgåssss/. It also gained its own plural ending (*-ar*) as opposed to *gås* which turns into *gäss* (geese) in plural. A typical example when it comes to compounds becoming words in their own right.

Trädgård (garden) also had its vowel(s) shortened and consonants prolonged: /träggggårrdd/.

Matsäck (brought food) is often pronounced /massssäck/ and doesn't make you think of a bag of food but rather a sandwich wrapped in aluminium foil and a juice box that you bring on a hike.

As with everything in this book, these things vary throughout dialects and among individual speakers.

115 The past tense of *stå* (to stand) is *stod* but **it's almost exclusively pronounced /stoooog/** – with a final *g* sound. Weird.

---

milk in a butter churn. Eventually people started to use it for a slice of bread with butter.

Confusing Things

116   Prepositions, prepositions, prepositions. One of the most difficult things to get right is the abstract use of prepositions. Rule number one when it comes to these little words is to understand that every language uses them differently and they are just as confusing in Swedish as they are in English or any other language.

Jag talar **i** telefon. – I'm **on** the phone.
(lit. "I'm speaking into the telephone.")

Even though you're not physically on top of a phone, English uses the preposition *on* here. In the Swedish sentence, we're speaking into the phone. Which seems to be more logical to you in terms of prepositions?

117   *På* is the preposition that, in my experience, confuses learners the most.

1. When used literally, it is very straightforward.

Boken ligger **på** bordet. – The book is **on** the table.

The following expressions are a bit of an in-betweener, since we're literally talking about being on top of something, but are at the same time talking about a place or institution (see point 4).

Jag är på Medborgarplatsen. – I'm at Medborgarplatsen.

Jag är på Island[1]. – I'm in Iceland.

Vi är på plats. – We're in place/we're there.

2. It's also used in a semi-abstract way, where an item is attached to another item without being on top.

Tavlan hänger på väggen. – The painting is hanging on the wall.

Polisen knackade på dörren. – The police knocked on the door.

Stjärnorna på himlen. – The stars in the sky.

3. However, this preposition is a part of a bunch of particle verbs, as a connector in front of a regular verb's object and in other expressions in a generic and abstract way or with a transferred meaning.

Hon tittar på tv. – She is watching TV.

Elektrikern slog på strömmen. – The electrician turned on the power.

Han hälsade på sin bror. – He visited his brother.

Jag tror på dig. – I believe in you.

Är du arg på mig? – Are you angry with me?

---

[1] Since Iceland is mostly seen as a big island, it's common to use *på* instead of *i* (which generally should be used with a country's name).

Hon väntar på honom. – She's waiting for him.

Det betyder "katt" på engelska. – It means "cat" in English.

Lita på mig! – Trust me!

Hunden såg på valpen. – The dog looked at the puppy.

Det var bara på låtsas. – It was just pretend.

Nu är det på allvar. – It's serious now.

Han jobbade på föredraget. – He worked on the presentation.

Hon spottade på rektorn. – She spit on the principal.

Det var på håret! – That was close!

4. When something is located or takes place in a kind of institution, *på* is used, when sometimes *i* (in) would be expected by the learner.

Vi går/är på [bio, teater, konsert]. – We're going to/are at the [cinema, theater, concert].

Jag är på [name of store, restaurant, club, bar]. – I'm at [name of store, restaurant, club, bar].

Det finns en på [street]. – There is one on [street].

Hon går på [school name]. – She's attending [school name].

Jag är på banken. – I'm at the bank.

Vi är på/måste <u>gå på</u> [tåget, bussen, båten, flyget]. – We are on/have to enter the [train, bus, ship, flight].

Det är tyst på biblioteket. – It's quiet at the library.

5. The preposition *på* is also used in a bunch of temporal expressions, mostly a definite point in time.

på måndag	on Monday
på måndagen	on the Monday
på måndagar	on Mondays
på morgonen	in the morning
på sommaren	in the summer
på natten	in the night
på kvällen	in the evening
på julen	at Christmas

6. Temporal expressions that express a time span in a negated sentence, also use *på*.

Jag har inte ätit på två dagar. – I haven't eaten in two days.

7. *På* can be used after verbs to signify that the action keeps being performed diligently. It's important that the stress lies on *på*.

Han <u>jobbade på</u>. – He kept on working.

Hon <u>tränade på</u>. – She kept on exercising.

Man får <u>kämpa på</u>. – One has to hang in.

8. It's also used when the result of an action emerges little by little, as a kind of present continuous tense.

Han jobbade på föredraget. – He was working on the presentation.
(Do you recognize this one? Context decides if he was a part of a team that worked on the presentation or if he was working on the presentation, doing some work.)

Hon åt på glassen. – She was eating her ice cream.

Flickan målar på sin bild. – The girl is painting her picture.

118 A preposition which is often confused with *på* in its abstract use is the preposition *i* (in).

1. It is used in its most basic form when talking about something being inside of something.

Jag är i huset. – I'm in the house.

2. Besides its basic meaning in a bunch of particle verbs, it's used as a connector between verb and object and in other abstract ways.

Du måste <u>ta i</u>! – You have to use all your strength!

Han <u>ramlade i</u>. – He fell in.

Han ramlade i trappan. – He fell on the stairs.

Hon hoppar i sängen. – She is jumping on the bed.

Jag ligger i sängen. – I'm lying in bed.

Hon <u>hoppade i</u>. – She jumped in.

Jag har bra betyg i svenska. – I have a good grade in Swedish.

i stället/istället – instead

3. As opposed to *på*, which is used when talking about being *at* or *in* an institution, *i* is used in a more tangible way in this scenario. Normally it's used when emphasizing being inside the actual building.

Jag är på bio. – I'm at the movies.

Jag är i bion. – I'm inside the cinema.

Jag är på [store name]. – I'm at [store name].

Jag är i affären. – I'm inside the store.

Jag är på tåget. – I'm on the train.

Jag är i tåget. – I'm inside the train.

Often *i* is preceded by *inne* (inside) to stress this even further: *jag är inne i tåget*.

4. *I* is used with temporal adverbials, I mean, ugh, phrases

expressing time.

i dag[2]	today
i går	yesterday
i morgon	tomorrow
i morgon bitti	tomorrow morning
i morse	this morning
i kväll	tonight
i helgen	next/last weekend (the tense will tell you which weekend it was)
i natt	last night/tonight
i sommar	this summer
i somras	last summer
i fjol[3]	last year
i jul	on Christmas
i julas	last Christmas

---

[2] Several of these kinds of prepositional words can be written as one or two words (*idag*, *igår*, *imorgon*). The key is to be consistent. If you decide to write *i dag*, you should also write *i går* and not mix. The same goes for words like *i stället/istället* (instead).

[3] Step up your game using *i fjol/ifjol* instead of *förra året*.

5. Where *på* is used for the future, *i* is used for the past, except for when it isn't (compare *i sommar – i somras* above).

Past	Future
i måndags – last Monday	på måndag – on Monday

6. When talking about a time span, *i* is used in an affirmative sentence (whereas *på* is used in a negated ditto).

Jag har bott här i tre år. – I've been living here for three years.

Jag har inte bott här på tre år. – I've not lived here in three years.

119 Learners often have problems with the preposition *om*, mostly because it's also a subjunction and an adverb, making it confusing to see the same word in so many different scenarios.

1. The preposition *om* means *around*, *beside* and *about*.

Han läser om andra världskriget. – He's reading about the Second World War.

Sverige ligger väster om Finland. – Sweden is located west of Finland.

Hon hade ett fint skärp om midjan. – She had a nice belt around her waist.

De hade knutit snöre om händerna på honom. – They had

tied a cord around his hands.

2. The adverb is used in particle verbs to mean that something needs to be done over again, like the prefix *re-* in English, or, with verbs indicating movement, that something moved past an object. It often turns up together with *vända* (to turn).

Jag <u>körde om</u> lastbilen. – I overtook the truck.

Hon <u>läste om</u> boken för andra gången. – She reread the book for the second time.

Löparen <u>sprang om</u> motståndaren. – The runner ran past the competition.

Vi måste <u>vända om</u>. – We have to go back.

3. And together with other verbs and in random particle verbs.

Polisen <u>talade om</u> för honom att det var fel. – The police explained to him that it was wrong.

Jag slår vad om att jag har rätt. – I bet that I'm right.

Det är väl inget att bråka om. – That's nothing to be fighting over, is it?

De tävlade om en ny cykel. – They were competing for a new bicycle.

En vän <u>sköter om</u> min trädgård. – A friend takes care of my garden.

4. *Om* is also used to express a time in which something is done a certain amount of times.

Hon äter tre gånger om dagen. – She eats three times a day.

En gång om året går han till tandläkaren. – Once a year he goes to the dentist.

5. It's used to express a duration of time before something will occur, equivalent to *in* in English.

Vi ses om en vecka. – See you in a week.

Jag kommer om en stund. – I'll come in a bit.

6. As a subjunction, it just means *if*. No surprises there.

Jag undrar om du vill ses. – I wonder if you want to meet.

Om det brinner, ring 112. – If there's a fire, call 112.

120 Some adverbs and prepositions come in two variants. These usually mean the same thing but might have some practical differences.

Mot and *emot* (against, towards) essentially mean the same thing and can be interchangeable, although *mot* is more common. When the preceding word ends on a consonant and when used in particle verbs, *emot* is usually chosen.

Är du mot(/emot) demokrati? – Are you against democracy?

Jag gick (mot/)emot dörren. – I walked towards/against the door.

Jag <u>slog emot</u> bilen med knät. – I walked into the car with my knee.

121 *Från* and *ifrån* (from) work similarly. There is no difference when using the words stand alone. However, in particle verbs only *ifrån* is used, as well as a suffix in compounds.

Från, on the other hand, can be used as a prefix in the same manner. This causes a particle verb to use *ifrån* where the particle isn't joined with the verb and *från* when it is (as is the case with the participle and some cases of infinitive).

Jag är från/ifrån Stockholm. – I'm from Stockholm.

Han kom gående från/ifrån affären. – He came walking from the store.

De <u>åkte ifrån</u> honom. – They went without him.
(lit. "They went from him.")

Han blev <u>frånåkt</u>. – He was left.
(lit. "He was gone from.")

122 *Utav* and *uti* (which mostly seems to occur in old songs) are casual variants of *av* (of) and *i* (in). These are not recommended in written Swedish, despite what many Swedes think. Furthermore, *utav* and *uti* can only be used as prepositions, whereas *av* and *i* are also adverbs. *Utifrån* is a similar word but is not considered informal.

Bordet är gjort utav/av trä. – The table is made out of wood[4].

Till marknaden uti Nora. – To the market in Nora.

Don't confuse *uti* with *ut i* or *ute i* which means *outside into* or *outside in*.

Vi går ut i skogen. – We're going outside into the forest.

Vi är ute i skogen. – We're outside in the forest.

123 The two Swedish grammatical genders can be confusing at first. It's hard to know when to use which one and this is something a lot of people struggle with. The words *planen* and *planet* both look like the same word in the definite form, where however *plan* (field) is an *en* word, *planet* (planet) also is an *en* word, but *plan* (plane) is an *ett* word.

There are a few pointers that can give you a hint about which grammatical gender to choose, but there is no fail-proof way of knowing and it's just something the learner has to deal with. Most words are *en* words, so the best thing is to try and see *ett* words as the exception that has to be focused on. Try to learn the genders together with the words, and if you spot a word, the plural ending could give you a hint.

No handbook without guidelines, so here we go:

---

[4] Compare the English translation. What do you see?

En

– About 75% of all nouns in Swedish

– People and animals have a tendency to be *en* words: *en flicka* (a girl), *en pojke* (a boy), *en man* (a man), *en kvinna* (a woman), *en skomakare* (a shoemaker), *en frisör* (a hairdresser), *en hund* (a dog), *en katt* (a cat), *en gris* (a pig), *en häst* (a horse).

– Days (because the ending *-dag* being an *en* word), months, seasons, and holidays: *en måndag* (a monday), *en maj* (a May), *en vinter* (a winter), *en jul* (a Christmas)

– The following endings **tend to be** *en* words: *-a, -an, -are, -dom, -else, -het, -ing, -lek, -nad,* and *-skap* as well as words borrowed from other languages with *-ett, -fon, -ik, -in, -ion, -ism, -ur,* and *-å*

I recommend that you forget all about this, and try to learn to distinguish *ett* words instead, since they are the exception.

Ett

– About 25% of all nouns in Swedish (obviously)

– Derogatory terms for people: *ett äckel* (a creep), *ett as* (an asshole), *ett luder* (a whore)

– Despite the rule about animals being *en* words, the word *djur* (animal) is not and thus logically all compounds with *-djur* aren't: *ett rådjur* (a deer), *ett näbbdjur* (a platypus)

– Continents, countries, regions, cities, villages, islands[5]: *ett*

---

[5] Yes, you guessed it: toponyms.

Amerika (an America), *ett Tyskland* (a Germany), *ett Stockholm*, *ett Löttorp*, *ett Värmdö*
– The endings *-age, -eri, -ori, -em, -gram, -iv, -ment, -skop, -tek,* and *-um*

Remember that there is mostly no real rule, except that a compound gets the same gender as its last word.

124 A few nouns exist in both genders: *en/ett paraply* (an umbrella). However they are few and nothing to worry too much about.

The really important part is the uncountable nouns where the meaning slightly changes depending on the gender.

Jag har köpt ett öl från Belgien. – I've bought a beer from Belgium.

Kan jag få en öl till? – Could I have another beer?

When talking about a kind or brand or kind of beer, it automagically turns into an *ett* word. When talking about a portion (a glass, bottle, bucket), the word is referred to as an *en* word.

The same goes for e.g. *kaffe* (coffee) or *vatten* (water).

Jag har köpt ett kaffe från Colombia. – I've bought a coffee from Colombia.

En kaffe, tack. – One coffee, please.

125   The Scandinavian languages are unique in that they use suffixes to construct the definite form of nouns as opposed to articles like in English (the), German (der, die, das), French (le, la) or Arabic (al) for instance.

This causes the learner to sometimes use the demonstrative pronoun *den* (for *en* words) and *det* (for *ett* words) to construct the definite form. In this case these articles can be translated as *that*, but needs to be followed by the **actual** definite form.

den bilen – **that** car

det huset – **that** house

Another use case for these articles is the double definite form used together with adjectives.
▷ **5, the double definite**

These articles are also used as determinative pronouns in a nominal phrase and are then followed by the indefinite form of the noun. This is used in conjunction with a relative clause. **I know, I know, lots of fancy talk but here is an example:**

Det första hus som jag ser köper jag. – The first house I see, I'll buy.

Det första hus is the subject here, followed by a clause that has a connection to the subject of the main clause. It is however common to use the definite form in spoken Swedish.

It can be hard to know when to use which but there are small differences in nuance if you consider this sentence:

Det huset som jag vill ha. – The house I want.
(This house exists.)

Det hus som jag vill ha. – The house I want.
(This is a potential house.)

All these use-cases also work in plural with the plural pronoun *de* (they).

126 Some English loan words in Swedish originate in the plural form. This means that they end on an *-s* although the singular is meant.

en muffins – a muffin

en keps – a cap
(e.g. baseball cap)

ett chips – a chip
(the snack)

en potatis – a potato

127 The general *det* (and sometimes *den*) can be a real struggle for learners. Oftentimes, when seemingly referring back to a noun, *det* is used regardless of grammatical gender.

1. Since Swedish places known information first in the sentence and new information tends to go at the end, we often use the general *det* to start sentences. That's why *det* is

used so, so much in Swedish to initiate a sentence because it acts as a placeholder for something known. It just needs to be there.

Det är en trevlig dag. – It's a nice day.

Det var inte jag. – It wasn't me.

Det står en bil i garaget. – There is a car in the garage.

Idag är det söndag. – It's Sunday today.
(Information that is emphasized may come in the first position of a sentence.)

2. *Det* can also be used as a placeholder to refer back to old information and to prepare us for new information.

– Vi kan gå på bio! (We could go to the movies!)
– Ja, det gör vi! (Yes, let's do that!)

3. When a verb just needs a subject, *det* is used.

Det kommer gäster senare. – We're having guests later.

Det snöar. – It's snowing.

Den is often used to refer to animate objects like animals (and, to a lesser extent, even people) even though the grammatical gender might be *ett*. The reason is that the historical masculine and feminine grammatical genders merged into what are *en* words today. It sounds more compassionate, humanizing if you will, towards animals and people to refer to them in this way, because there's a risk that it could sound like they're seen as inanimate things. If the sex is known, *han* (he) or *hon* (she) is usually used.

Ser du lejonet där borta? Han/hon/den är skadad. – Do you see the lion over there? He/she/it is hurt.

128 Swedish is one of few languages (if not the only[6]) where the helper verb *ha* (to have) can be dropped in the perfect and past perfect tense. This is done, either after another helper verb or in a subordinate clause.

Jag måste (ha) tappat den. – I must have lost it.

Jag är ledsen eftersom jag (har) tappat den. – I'm sad because I've lost it.

Den försvann efter att jag (hade) lagt den någonstans. – It disappeared after I had put it somewhere.

129 Another word that can be omitted is *som*. The sentence we took a look at earlier will thus be:

Det första hus (som) jag ser köper jag. – The first house (that) I see, I'll buy.

This is only possible if the relative clause (*som jag ser*) has a subject (*jag*) of its own.

Det första hus som är rött. – The first house that is red.

---

[6] It was borrowed from German during the time of the Swedish Empire in the 1600s, but has since been actively phased out by German grammaticians. Swedes developed this phenomenon further instead. Happy days.

130   When a sentence expresses direction (e.g. with *till*, *åt* or an adverb), the main verb (*gå*, *åka*, etc.) can be dropped if one of the helper verbs *skola*, *måste*, or *vilja* is present. The preposition makes the context clear.

Jag ska till affären. – I'm going to the store.

Du måste till doktorn. – I have to go to the doctor.

131   *Skola* is a curious verb. It can be used in so many ways that it can be hard for the learner to distinguish exactly what's meant.

1. The present tense *ska* is used to indicate the future tense. The past tense form *skulle* references to the future in the past.
▷ **29, future tense with *skola***

Jag ska städa mitt rum. – I will be cleaning my room.

Jag skulle städa mitt rum när... – I was about to clean my room, when...

2. Using the future tense with *ska* can sound like an order, frequently practiced by parents.

Du ska städa ditt rum nu. – You're going to clean your room now.

Putting the stress on the verb (*städa*), or the object (*ditt rum*) when there is one present, means that this is new information or slightly weakens the order. Putting the stress on *ska* makes the order stronger and as if the receiver already knew and hasn't acted on it.

3. If a piece of information is coming from a third party, *ska* is used to indicate that. This often goes together with *tydligen* (apparently) to weaken the statement and the speaker's accountability.

De ska (tydligen) gifta sig (har jag hört). – They're (apparently) getting married (or so I've heard).

Han ska ha dödat honom. – (Apparently) he killed him.

4. The past tense form *skulle* is used to express possible or non-real events also known as the past subjunctive mood.
▷ **41, the past subjunctive mood**

Det skulle vara bra. – It would be good.

132 *Få* is one of my favorite Swedish words due to the sheer amount of meanings it can have, some of which are hard to translate.

1. The most basic translation of *få* is *to receive*.

Jag fick den i julklapp. – I got it for Christmas.

Kan jag få pennan? – Can I have the pen?

Han fick en örfil. – He was slapped.

Du får en puss om du hjälper mig. – You'll get a kiss if you help me.

Vad får vi till middag? – What are we getting for dinner?

2. The next, still pretty basic translation, is *to be allowed*. It is also used in a weakened manner of being allowed when talking about senses.

Får jag gå från bordet? – May I leave the table?

Man får röka här. – It's allowed to smoke here.

Barn får inte vara uppe för sent. – Children mustn't be up too late.

Men jag får. – But I'm allowed to.

Du får se vad som händer. – You'll see what will happen.

Nu ska ni få höra. – I've got something to tell you.
(lit. "Now you'll get to hear.")

3. Now we're getting to the good bits. The verb can be translated as *to have to*, which is confusing to many people.

Nu får du vara tyst! – Now be quiet!

Vi fick vänta 40 minuter på maten. – We had to wait 40 minutes for our food.

Få and *måste* can be synonyms here but where they differ is that *måste* expresses that there is some party involved that actively forces the subject into action whereas *få* relies on more external circumstances. The conditions are basically softer and rely more on the subject's own willingness. *Måste* could also be used in this sense depending on the speaker.

This guideline is somewhat blurry, as most linguistic guidelines are, but it's as good as any.

Jag måste gå till skolan imorgon. – I must go to school tomorrow.
(I'm obligated to by law.)

Jag får gå till skolan imorgon. – (I guess) I have to go to school tomorrow.
(Because I mistakenly left my bag in my locker.)

It is also used in a weaker sense to express a reason to have to do something. In this case, *måste* is often used in conjunction with *få* to emphasize an urge that the speaker has.

Jag måste få säga hur fin du är idag. – I just have to say how nice you look today.

Jag får tacka så mycket. – Thank you so much.
(lit. "I must thank so much.")

4. When trying to affect someone into action, we can use *få* as a translation for *to get*.

Vi måste få honom att prata. – We have to get him to speak.

5. Finally we have my favorite translation which is *to suddenly experience something with your senses* or *to suddenly get to know something*.

Han fick se henne sitta ensam på bänken. – He suddenly

saw her sitting alone on the bench.

Plötsligt fick de höra sirener. – Suddenly they heard sirens.

Jag fick just veta att jag vunnit. – I just heard that I won.

133 *Böra* (should) is commonly used either in its present tense *bör* or even more commonly in the past tense, or rather the subjunctive mood, *borde*. As we know, that mood is a bit sneaky in Swedish.

All you need to know is that *borde* is the most common one, expressing a suggestion and with a subtle dash of opinion, whereas *bör* gives it a more official and pressing tone, mostly used, but not exclusively, in writing. This turns it into an "it's your choice but there will be consequences" kind of expression instead of "you should because I think so".

Du borde duscha. – You should take a shower.

Alla borde läsa Bibeln. – Everyone should read the Bible.

Du bör läsa igenom dokumenten. – You should read through the documents.

Man bör inte gå naken på gatan. – One shouldn't walk naked in the street.

134 The helper verb *kunna* is used to express someone's ability to do something or to make a request.

Hon kan stå på händer. – She can do a handstand.

Kan du hjälpa mig? – Could you help me?

But the confusing part is that *kunna* is also used for expressing having knowledge about a particular subject. This would be translated as *to know* in English.

Jag kan svenska. – I know Swedish.

Han kan multiplikationstabellen. – He knows the multiplication table.

Kan du japanska? – Do you know Japanese?

Hon kan svenska nationalsången. – She knows the Swedish national anthem.

135 Two common verbs have gotten their past tense shortened. The longer forms are now considered to have a more formal and/or literary style and are virtually never used in spoken Swedish.

The words in question are *lägga* (to put) and *säga* (to say), which have both the short variants, *la* (put) and *sa* (said), as well as the long variants, *lade* and *sade*, in the past tense. *Lade* still remains the most common variant in writing whereas reading a book, you'll definitely come across both past tense variants of *säga*. I swear on my collection of grammar books.

136 Another set of verbs has a shortened infinitive and present tense form. These are already ranked as old and dusty but could be good to know anyway: *taga* (to take), *hava* (to have), *bliva* (to become), *draga* (to pull).

The contemporary forms, which should be used in all styles of text, are: *ta*, *ha*, *bli*, and *dra*.

137 Sometimes the past tense is used when something is actually happening in the present. This is done when the speaker adds an opinion into the mix. Some people think that this sounds super weird.

Det här var gott! – This is (was) delicious!

Det här var jobbigt! – This is (was) exhausting!

138 When an item is located somewhere, its orientation is made clear by using the verbs *stå* (to stand), *ligga* (to lie), and *sitta* (to sit). This is however often just translated to *to be* in English.

Boken står i hyllan. – The book is on the shelf.

Boken ligger på bordet. – The book is on the table.

Affischen sitter på väggen. – The poster is on the wall.

139 Furthermore, when putting something somewhere, the verbs *ställa*, *lägga*, and *sätta* are used. These are translated to *to put* and the orientations correspond to those of their counterparts mentioned above.
▷ **138, *stå, ligga, sitta***

Jag ställer boken i hyllan. – I'm putting the book on the shelf. *(in a standing position)*

Jag lägger boken på bordet. – I'm putting the book on the

table.
(in a lying position)

Jag sätter affischen på väggen. – I'm putting the poster on the wall.
(sticking it (in)to something)

140 Some verbs have both a weak and a strong conjugation (belonging to both the second and the fourth conjugation group). The reasons for this are many: some may be archaic forms, some may be regional, some co-exist beside each other in standard Swedish and some have slightly different meanings.

The usage of the following examples fluctuate somewhat, so they are to be taken with a grain of salt. For instance, according to SAOL[7], the variant of the verb in the fourth conjugation group can take the meanings of both variants. The usage can vary among speakers, regions or even within one's individual language.

Fourth conjugation group	Second conjugation group
frysa (to feel cold, to turn to ice)	frysa (to get something to freeze)
smälta (to melt)	smälta (to get something to melt)
lysa (to be lit) (regional)	lysa (to be lit)

---

[7] Svenska Akademiens ordlista (The glossary of the Swedish Academy)

The differences are visible only in the past tense.

Jag fryste kycklingen. – I froze the chicken.

Jag frös. – I was freezing.

Sjön frös till is. – The lake turned (froze) to ice.

Solen smälte glassen. – The sun melted the ice cream.

Glassen smalt. – The ice cream melted.

Lampan lyste. – The lamp was lit.

Lampan lös. – The lamp was lit.

141 If a question is negated, you don't answer *ja* (yes) but *jo* (yes) if you want to contradict it.

– Är han inte hemma? (Isn't he at home?)
– Jo, det är han! (Yes, he is!)

This extra word is also colloquially used in place of the general *ja*.

– Sover du? (Are you asleep?)
– Jo... (Yeah...)

142 Responding to statements with *ja* (yes) or *nej* (no) is also confusing in Swedish, since it differs a bit from other languages.

When the statement is affirmative, the answer is *ja* for agreeing and *nej* for disagreeing.

– Maten är god. (The food is delicious.)
– Ja, det är den. (Yes, it is.)
– Nej, det är den inte. (No, it isn't.)

When, however, the statement is negative, you answer *nej* for agreeing and *jo* for disagreeing.

– Maten är inte god. (The food isn't delicious.)
– Nej, det är den inte. (Yes/No, it isn't.)
– Jo, det är den. (No, it is.)

In other languages different from Swedish, it's common to answer *yes* when agreeing to the negated statement, which can be quite confusing.

143 Even though a word stands in its singular form, it can act as plural if it's referring to a group of things or people in real life[8]. This is called semantic congruence. Not that you needed to know that.

In Swedish, this is made visible by an adjective being declined in the plural instead of the singular.

Personalen var trevliga på båten. – The staff was ("were") nice on the ship.

---

[8] Compare this to British English "The parliament have voted."

Polisen[9] var nöjda med tillslaget. – The police was ("were") satisfied with the raid.

144 *Inte* (no) is a negation that changes places depending on the type of clause.

In main clauses, *inte* goes after the finite verb. The conjugated verb, that is.

Jag gillar **inte** strumpor. – I don't like socks.

Du måste **inte** gilla strumpor. – You don't have to like socks.

In subordinate clauses, it has to sit in front of the finite verb.

Eftersom jag **inte** gillar strumpor. – Because I don't like socks.

However, if the verb comes with an unstressed pronoun, *inte* can come after it instead.

Jag hatar dig **inte**. – I don't hate you.

Ät den **inte**! – Don't eat it!

The name for this is the *Biff*[10] rule and is valid for sentence adverbials in general. These are words and phrases that modify the whole sentence.

---

[9] In Swedish, the authority *Polisen* is a singular word. The plural would refer to individual police officers.

[10] I **b**isats kommer *inte* **f**öre det **f**örsta verbet.

Jag är **ju** svensk. – I'm Swedish you know.

Han är **verkligen** snäll. – He's really kind.

De är **väl** trötta. – I guess they're tired.

Eftersom jag **ju** är svensk. – Because I'm Swedish you know.

Eftersom han **verkligen** är snäll. – Because he's really kind.

Eftersom de **väl** är trötta. – Because they're tired I guess.

Remember that the particle of a particle verb isn't seen as a part of the verb in this regard. Therefore *inte* has to be placed in-between when it should be located after the verb.

<u>Hälsa</u> **inte** <u>på</u> mer! – Don't visit anymore!

145 When listening to Swedish or engaging in a conversation you might come across doubling of the negation or pronoun to put some extra emphasis on those[11]. This is considered dialectal and nothing you have to do, but since you'll probably come across it, it's good to know about.

Inte jag, inte. – Not me.
(*No sir!*)

Han är snygg, han. – He's good-looking.
(*He really is.*)

---

[11] Compare this to how some English dialects use doubling too, e.g. "He's a good-looking fellow, he is."

146 *Också* (also, too) is replaced by *heller* (neither) in negated sentences.

Jag har också en sådan. – I also have one.

Jag har inte heller en sådan. – I don't have one either.

147 The pronoun *egen* (own) is often treated as an adjective. This is very common in spoken Swedish and will probably make its way into more formal texts sooner or later.

Egen, eget, egna are used for nouns in the indefinite form, and *egna* for the definite form. This is what makes it look like an adjective.

en egen bil – (one's) own car

ett eget hus – (one's) own house

egna bilar – (one's) own cars

den egna bilen – (one's) own car

det egna huset – (one's) own house

de egna bilarna – (one's) own cars

So good so far, but as you can see, Swedish makes a difference between the definite and indefinite form here.

After possessive pronouns, **this declension is also supposed to be used**. This is where spoken Swedish often differs from standard written Swedish[12].

min egen bil – my own car

mitt eget hus – my own house

mina egna bilar – my own cars

In spoken Swedish, this is treated like an adjective where the definite form and the possessive form are the same.

min **egna** bil – my own car

mitt **egna** hus – my own house

mina **egna** bilar – my own cars

In standard written Swedish, however, *egna* is used when a word stands between it and the pronoun.

min stora egna bil – my big own car

mitt stora egna hus – my big own house

148 The definite and plural variants of the colors *blå* (blue) and *grå* (gray) can either be *blå/grå* or *blåa/gråa*.

The words were originally *blaa* and *graa* but double *a* eventually merged into an *å* and people later forgot how the words were initially pronounced. They started to construct a

---

[12] The "standard written Swedish" is of course also used by people in spoken Swedish.

new plural form analogous to other adjectives that usually end on an -*a*.

Both variants are considered equally correct.

149 Some adjectives are, what linguists call, *defective*. This means that they are missing certain forms. In Swedish, there are a bunch of words like this that lack the form for *ett* words.

Hunden är rädd. – The dog is afraid.

Festen var kul[13]. – The party was fun.

Jag är lat. – I'm lazy.

Hon är så pryd. – She is so prudish.

~~Barnet är rätt. – The child is afraid.~~

~~Evenemanget var kult. – The event was fun.~~

~~Barnet är latt. – The child is lazy.~~

~~Hembiträdet är prytt. – The maid is prudis.~~

If you have *ett lejon* (a lion) that is afraid, you have to rephrase the sentence. There is no other way around that. An example is to replace the noun with *han*, *hon* or *den* (depending on if the animal's sex is known).

---

[13] *Kul* can always be used uninflected but since it lacks an obvious plural form, *kuliga* has emerged in colloquial Swedish.

I know what you're thinking, but *den* is often used as a placeholder when talking about animals and people (regardless of their grammatical gender).

▷ **127, the general *det***

150 The pronouns *vår/vårt* (our) and *er/ert* (your, plural) are often pronounced *våran/vårat* and *eran/erat* which has its origin in the old masculine accusative form of the words.

This will also frequently turn up in casual texts.

151 The Swedish word for *small* (liten/litet) can seem complicated due to its several different forms.

The indefinite form follows the regular pattern for adjectives and probably reminds you of the English word *little*.

en liten bil – a small car

ett litet hus – a small house

The definite form is *lilla* and differs from the plural form in this case.

den lilla bilen – the small car

det lilla huset – the small house

The plural form is *små* which I'm sure reminds you of *small*.

små bilar – small cars

små hus – small houses

de små bilarna – the small cars

de små husen – the small houses

To top it off, the comparative forms are *mindre/minst* and are totally irregular.

Bilen är mindre än huset. – The car is smaller than the house.

Huset är minst. – The house is the smallest.

152 *Lite* (originally *litet*) can mean both *little* and *some*, which can cause a change in meaning if you don't pay attention. There is also a difference in stress.

Jag äter lite mat. /ja äter LIIIITE mat/ – I eat little food. *(in general)*

Jag äter lite mat. /ja äter lite MAAAAT/ – I'm eating some food.

153 When there's a need to translate *another* or *other* into Swedish, there are a few options to consider. As always, this can be confusing to the learner, so let's break it down together.

1. *Annan* means *another* but in the context of *different*.

Nej, jag vill ha en annan. – No, I want a different one.

Vi gör det en annan dag. – Let's do that another day.

Kan du ge mig en annan penna? – Can you give me a

different pen?

I ett annat[14] liv kanske. – In another life perhaps.

2. Andra really means *second* but can be used in some cases where we would use *other* in English. **It can, however, also be the plural form of *annan.***

Alla andra tittade på. – All the others were watching.

Det känns som ett andra hem. – It feels like a second home.

Han behöver andra skor. – He needs other shoes.

Har du andra planer? – Do you have different plans?

3. When talking about *another* in the meaning *an additional something*, we can use *till*. It can stand either after the indefinite article (*en/ett*) or at the end of the sentence.

Vill du ha en till smörgås? – Do you want another sandwich?

De dricker en kopp kaffe till. – They are drinking another cup of coffee.

Jag ska köpa en till bil. – I'm going to buy another car.

Hon stannade en dag till. – She stayed another day.

---

[14] *Annan* also has to be declined according to the grammatical gender and number.

Old Swedish Relics

154   Swedish is a language riddled with relics from a gone-by era, which a native Swede could have a problem explaining. These are things you just say because they've always been said and no one yet started to say them differently.

One of these things is the use of the possessive case after the preposition *till* (to). This is still practiced regularly in Icelandic but only in certain frozen expressions in Swedish.

till sängs	to bed
till skogs	into the forest
till sjöss	at sea
till havs	at sea
till lands	on land
till salu	for sale (old possessive form)
till döds	to death
till hands	at hand
till låns	on loan
till freds	satisfied

155 You're taught that *honom* (him) is the object form of *han* (he) but what you might not know is that *han* is also the former accusative form which makes it a very common occurrence in spoken Swedish in place of *honom*.

Purists consider this to be wrong, in spite of the fact that it's a more correct option, historically. Remember, written language is the exception and doesn't always reflect the alive and wild spoken language.

It's super common and if you feel like taking a step into a more native approach, you could try it out.

Jag såg han i affären i dag. – I saw him in the store today.

156 Related to the above are the contractions *'an* (him) and *'na* (her) which exist in several dialects. These are related to the old accusative forms *han* (him) and *hana* (her). As a reminder, the standard Swedish forms were *honom* (him) and *henne* (her) from the old dative forms.

Har du sett'na? – Have you seen her?

Var är'an? – Where is he?

157 If you have seen the preposition *å*, you should know that it's the same word as *på*. During the Middle Ages some peasants got unsure where the word boundary in *uppå* (upon) was – or something – and started to pronounce *å* as *på* instead. Today *å* still lives on in some set phrases and in somewhat formal language.

å ena sidan – on one hand

å andra sidan – on the other hand

å företagets vägnar – on behalf of the company

158 There are set phrases using the old present subjunctive mood. You don't need to know how this works (it's mostly the verb stem + the suffix -*e*) but the expressions are good to know.

▷ **40, the present subjunctive mood**

Det vete katten/fan. – God knows.
(lit. "The cat/devil may know")

Han leve! – May he live!

The adverb *vare sig* (neither, no matter if) originates in this verb form.

Vare sig jag eller du vet. – Neither you nor I know.

Vare sig han vill det eller inte. – No matter if he wants it or not.

159 The past subjunctive mood has generally merged with the regular past tense form but one single word still lives on. Just like in English, the word *vore* (were), which is the past subjunctive of *vara* (to be), is still being used frequently.

▷ **41, the past subjunctive mood**

Jag önskar att jag vore en kanin. – I wish that I were a rabbit.

160   The verb *bli* (to become) has replaced *varda* in contemporary Swedish but the past tense form *vart* still lives on in a number of dialects including my own. You will most definitely hear it, because of its use in the Stockholm area (and thus in a lot of media, sorry rural Sweden).

Det vart bra. – It turned out well.

Det blev bra. – It turned out well.

161   Personal verb conjugations disappeared from spoken Swedish a long time ago but lingered on until the mid-20th century in written Swedish. The Swedish news agency TT decided to drop the use of plural forms in 1945 and started a small linguistic revolution.

These were used with *vi* (we), *ni* (you), *de* (they), and, of course, any noun in plural. If you're reading a classic book, you will definitely have to battle these old forms.

Until fairly recently it also still existed on signs in this phrase *obehöriga äga ej tillträde* (no unauthorized entry) because the archaic language felt intimidating and authoritarian. The expression *därom tvista de lärde*[1] (the scholars argue about that) also uses the old plural verb form.

The plural form was identical to that of the infinitive, however the past tense of the verbs in the fourth conjugation group (the strong verbs) ended on an *-o*.

---

[1] The expression is used when something is particularly difficult to answer or solve.

Vi komma till Stockholm. – We are coming to Stockholm.

Fåglarna sjunga så vackert. – The birds are singing so beautifully.

De dogo av svält. – They died of starvation.

The verb *vara* (to be) tends to be an exception in all languages and this case is no exception (pun intended). The plural form was constructed by adding an *-o* to the singular *är*.

Barnen äro hungriga. – The children are hungry.

Another exception is the second person plural. The pronoun *ni* (you) is actually a contraction of the older second person plural suffix *-en* and the pronoun *I*. When they merged, the singular verb form started to be used.

Kommen I? – Are you coming?

Kommer ni? – Are you coming?

You'll probably never need this information, but what's a language handbook without a bit of fun facts?

162 Even though the masculine and feminine grammatical genders have merged into *en* words, the masculine adjective ending *-e* (used as an attribute) is still, but barely, clinging on to life. It's used as a semantic gender, where the sex is known. It's getting rarer and rarer by the minute.
▷ **42, adjectives**

den store kungen – the great king

den långe farbrorn[2] – the tall uncle

den snälle läkaren – the kind doctor

Even though we're singing its requiem, the masculine adjective ending is probably going to live on a bit longer in proper names.

Karl den store – Charles the Great

Johannes Paulus II (den andre) – John Paul II (the second)

Gustav II (den andre) Adolf – Gustav II (the second) Adolph

This is not to be confused with those ordinal numbers that always end on -e.

▷ **65, numbers**

163 The old accusative case doesn't only exist in personal pronouns but also in a bunch of set phrases. You can recognize them by the adjective ending -an.

stå i ljusan låga – ablaze
(lit. "to stand in bright flame")

i högan sky – high up in the sky

i rättan tid – just about time
(lit. "in right time")

---

[2] Also used for older men in general.

164 For the sake of being complete, let's take a look at some set phrases in the old dative case. You'll recognize them by the endings *-om*, *-e* and *-o*.

i sinom tid – in due time
(lit. "in its time")

gå man ur huse – go out en masse
(lit. "to walk man out of house")

skämt åsido – jokes aside

vara av ondo – to be bad
(lit. "to be of evil")

i blindo – blindly

på sistone[3] – lately
(lit. "on the late")

---

[3] *-ne* is an old definite suffix. You didn't need to know that.

Mistakes Even Swedes Make

165 Languages are evolving beings, thriving on mistakes and changes made by their native speakers. One of the most common mistakes in contemporary Swedish that is probably bound to become the norm one day is the interchanging of *var* (where) and *vart* (where to).

You are super likely to hear Swedes use *vart* in both cases.

166 The conjunction *även fast* (although) is a Frankenstein's monster thrown together from *fast* (although) and *även om* (although). You'll hear this one a lot but it should be avoided in formal texts.

167 The prepositions *innan* (before) and *före* (before) are often confused because they seem interchangeable. In reality, they only kind of are. *Före* can mean both *in front of* or *before* whereas *innan* only can be used with time. And this is where Swedes get confused themselves.

Han ställde sig före mig i kön. – He got in line in front of me.

Han ställde sig före mig i kön. – He got in line before me.

Han ställde sig innan mig i kön. – He got in line before me.

Furthermore, *innan* is a subjunction which *före* is not.

Vi måste gå innan det börjar regna. – We have to go before it starts to rain.

168 *Ni* (you, plural) is sometimes taught as the equivalent to the German *Sie*, the French *Vous*, or Spanish *Usted* – as a polite pronoun. It has in recent years started to gain popularity among young Swedes in service professions.

This is somewhat problematic, since it has **never been a polite pronoun**.

The shift started some 200 years ago where using *ni* was already considered too familiar. Swedes then started to use titles to show respect. Using *ni*, on the other hand, was a way to address title-less people, be it servants, employees or store clerks. They were then expected to reply back with e.g. *herr* (Mr.) or *fru* (Mrs.), with a professional title, a noble title, or an academic title. This could also be combined with a last name.

Even children, being addressed by adults with *du* (singular you) were expected to reply with titles to show respect.

The title had to be reused every time the person was addressed and a pronoun was not used, making this quite a complicated feat.

Önskar direktörn något att dricka eller vill direktörn kanske ha en bit mat i stället? – Does the manager wish something to drink or maybe the manager would like a bit of food instead?

If the title was unknown, complicated sentence constructions were used to avoid the need to address anyone at all, some of which live on today as common set phrases like *vad sägs om det här?* (How about this?) and *var det bra så?* (Is that all?).

Ni was only sporadically used between complete strangers or in ads, since they are supposed to address everyone.

▷ **277, addressing one person with the plural *ni***

Since the 1960s[1], Swedes have completely moved over to using the more familiar *du* and are on a first name basis with everyone. Yes, this includes bosses, teachers, police and the prime minister. The royal family is still being addressed by their titles – **but not *ni*.**

169 Depending on how you look at the world, Swedes use the words *mycket* (much)/*lite* (little) and *många* (many)/*få* (few) incorrectly.

The reason is that *mycket/lite* are supposed to be used for only uncountable things:

mycket/lite vatten – much/little water

mycket/lite choklad – much/little chocolate

många/få sniglar – many/few slugs

---

[1] This was, of course, a gradual change, but the turning point came in 1967 when the new Director General of the National Swedish Board of Health (*Medicinalstyrelsen*), Bror Rexed, asked his employees in a speech to call him Bror or *du*.

många/få människor – many/few people

But depending on how you see it, a lot of words in plural could be seen as an uncountable mass.

mycket/lite människor – much/few people

And this is why it's super common for Swedes to use this uncountable variant even for countable nouns.

170 Some Swedes tend to compare the adjective *dålig* (bad) in a regular manner, although it doesn't have a regular second and third degree: *dåligare, dåligast*.

This sounds rather childish and should be avoided.
▷ **205, *sämre*** ▷ **206, *värre***

171 It's extremely common in colloquial Swedish to add an *att* (that) after *eftersom* (because) and other subjunctions which don't require it. The culprit is likely *därför att* (because) and other similar subjunctions.

Eftersom att vi har bråttom. – Because we're in a hurry.

172 The reflexive possessive pronouns seem to be singing on the last chorus[2], as we say in Sweden. This error has even made its way into newspapers.

De tjänar pengar på deras youtubekanal. – They are making money off their YouTube channel.

---

[2] Sjunga på sista refrängen.

Both the third person singular and plural should make use of *sin*, *sitt*, or *sina* here.

▷ **60, reflexive possessive pronouns**

De tjänar pengar på sin youtubekanal. – They are making money off their (own) YouTube channel.

173 *Apropå* (apropos) is one of many French loan words in Swedish. This particular one has started transforming into the more Swedish looking *att bero på*. This is similar to the actually existing expression *det beror på* (it depends on).

I blame Swedes' love for reductions. Say *att bero på* quickly and it turns into /a bro påååå/ which sounds scary similar to *apropå*.

174 I was reluctant to put this one under "mistakes Swedes make", since it depends on how you analyze the grammar, but it's a fact that a lot of people like to fight about this. I'm talking about the word *än* (than) and what should come after it. A subject pronoun or an object pronoun?

Du är smartare än mig. – You're smarter than me.

Du är smartare än jag (är). – You're smarter than I (am).

Now, is *än* a preposition or a subjunction? This is definitely not a new discussion, a tale as old as time even in the Anglosphere, and in the end, the speakers decide and both variants are very much in use. No variant is considered more casual than the other in Swedish.

Polite Swedish

175 It's quite common for non-Swedes to think that Swedes are a casual people, being informal all the time which for some people can seem rather rude. This is only because they only think in terms of their own culture where you need to humble yourself with phrases that don't really mean anything and are only expected to be there.

This is obviously the wrong approach to take when looking at another culture. Swedes are a reserved people who value private space and avoid conflicts. Politeness is thus expressed with insecurity and vagueness, using long sentences and using exaggerated long syllables rather than with a set of distancing impersonal phrases.

People learning Swedish are so used to using a word like *please* that they try to force a *snälla* or a *tack* into every single request.

This is not really the way to go.

176 *Tack* really means *thanks* and is used like *please* in English, however when putting emphasis on it, it can sound impatient and rude, marking that you should already have received what you wanted, in which case you would normally say thanks. It's mostly used when ordering things but can often be omitted.

Instead we form our requests or orders as longer form questions, often giving the receiver room to say *yes* or *no* (although it is obviously inferred in certain situations (employer – boss relationship) that you have to accept).

Är du snäll och... – Would you be so kind and...

Har du något emot att... – Would you mind to...

Har du tid att... – Do you have time to...

Jag undrar om... – I wonder if...

The last expression can be used to make the request even more unreal and vague, turning it into a thought and making the sentence longer. It can be used with any of the other requests.

Jag undrar om du har något emot att... – I wonder if you would mind to...

177 *Skulle* can also be used to construct a longer and more vague sentence. The longer the more polite.

Skulle du kunna vara så snäll och... – (lit.) Would you be able to be so kind and...

Skulle du ha något emot att... – (lit.) Would you have anything against...

Skulle du ha tid att... – Would you have time to...

Together with *jag undrar om*, we can create a very long

tentative request.

Jag undrar om du skulle ha något emot att... – I wonder if
you would have anything against...

178 *Snälla* means *please*, from *snäll* (kind), and is used as a more
begging *please*.

Ursäkta, snälla, kan du hjälpa mig? – Excuse me, please,
could you help me?

Snälla pappa, jag kan väl få en glass? – Please daddy,
couldn't I have an ice cream, could I?

179 Another word commonly translated as *please* is *vänligen*
(kindly). It is mostly seen on signs and in formal written
Swedish to form a request.

Vänligen ta av er skorna vid ingången. – Please, take off
your shoes at the entrance.

Vänligen håll dörren stängd. – Please, keep the door closed.

Vänligen städa efter dig. – Please, clean up after yourself.

180 Despite not using an equivalent for *please* that often, Swedes
do compensate for that by thanking a lot. Thanking back
(*tack själv*), thanking for the last time you saw someone (*tack
för senast*), thanking for getting to borrow something (*tack
för lånet*), thanking for getting to see something (*tack för
titten*), etc.

181 The go-to answer to *tack* (thank you) is *var så god* (here you go) which literally means *be so kind*. It can of course also be used when actually handing someone something, prior to the thanking.

However there are also *ingen fara* (lit. "no danger"), *inga problem* (no problem), and *det var så lite, så* (lit. "it was so little, so").

Ingen fara and *inga problem* are also used as an answer to an excuse.

– Oj, ursäkta! (Oops, I'm sorry!)
– Det är ingen fara. (That's alright.)

182 One thing that makes a lot of people from other cultures cringe is the lack of a polite pronoun (Swedes use *du* with everyone) and the use of first names with strangers. This is completely normal in Sweden. The history behind this is quite fascinating.

▷ **168, the "polite" pronoun**

Vocabulary

183 A common misconception among learners is the meaning of *gå* (to go). Its primary meaning is actually *to walk* but could be used more abstractly like in the following cases:

Jag går i skolan. – I go to school.

Jag går på bio. – I'm going to the movies.

184 Instead of *lära sig* (to learn), people swap that out for *lära* (to teach), since the English counterpart isn't reflexive. In Swedish you are literally teaching yourself.

By the way, the present tense is *lär*, **not** *lärar*. Also a common mistake.

Jag lär mig svenska. – I'm learning Swedish.

Jag lär honom svenska. – I'm teaching him Swedish.

As a side note, *lära* (non-reflexive) could also mean *to learn* in a few cases.

Jag har lätt för att lära. – It's easy for me to learn new things.

Vi lärde känna varandra. – We got to know each other.

Lära also comes in the form of particle verbs: *lära in* (to learn) and *lära ut* (to teach).

Han <u>lärde in</u> manuset. – He learned the script.

Hon <u>lär ut</u> svenska på universitet. – She teaches Swedish at the university.

185   Adding *ihjäl* to a verb creates a particle verb that means the action was performed until someone died, both metaphorically and literally.

Hon <u>slog ihjäl</u> katten. – She beat the cat to death.

Han <u>stirrade ihjäl</u> mig. – He stared me to death.

Det känns som om jag just <u>åt ihjäl</u> mig. – It feels like I've just eaten myself to death.
(This refers to the amount of food that was eaten.)

186   *Leka* (to play) and *spela* (to play) have two slightly different meanings. *Leka* is something you do with toys and children's games. In certain contexts it can refer to someone using something in a non-serious manner.

leka kull – to play tag

leka brandman – to play fire fighter

leka med bilar – to play with cars

leka med prylar – to play with gadgets

leka med elden – to play with fire

Spela is used for games – games with rules that you can win – as opposed to children's games that are a bit looser put together.

spela fotboll – to play soccer[1]

spela monopol – to play monopoly

spela kort – to play cards

187 *Kille* (guy) and *tjej* (girl) are two colloquial words that can be confusing since it can be tricky to know when to use *pojke* (boy) and *flicka* (girl) which are more straightforward.

1. *Kille* and *tjej* are roughly used for teens, however there are just too many exceptions for this to be a real rule.

2. When middle-aged women call themselves *girls* in English, it's *tjejer*[2] in Swedish.

3. The words can also be translated as *boyfriend* and *girlfriend*.

4. Furthermore, they can be used when announcing the gender of a baby: *Det blev en liten kille/tjej!* (It's a boy/girl! lit. "It turned into a little boy/girl!"). In this way, a parent can also refer to their children even if they aren't babies.

Min stora kille gillar fotboll. – My big guy likes soccer.

Sorry to break it to you, but it's just not that easy to choose.

---

[1] Yes I know, but this book is written in American English.

[2] Where guys normally use *grabbar* (guys) or *gubbar* (old men).

188 *Kaka* (cookie) and *kex* (cracker) can be hard to distinguish. The rule of thumb is that a *kaka* is mostly sweet whereas a *kex* isn't. However, a *mariekex* (Marie biscuit) is a sweet biscuit.

A *kaka* could also be a cake that isn't layered (which would then be a *tårta*), like *sockerkaka* (sponge cake). It is also used to refer to a chocolate bar that is flat, usually divided into several squares. Those are called *chokladkaka* (chocolate bar). Some sorts of round bread are also referred to as *kaka* like *hönökaka*[3].

As a bonus, let's talk about *rån* (wafers). They can be small and sweet, layered with different types of fillings (like chocolate, vanilla and lemon). We don't call them *kaka* because of this – just *rån*. However, they can also be bigger and non-sweet, eaten with cheese. They then go in the *kex* drawer.

189 *Saft* and *juice* both mean *juice* in English but there are (sometimes) differences to regard. *Juice* is a beverage from pure fruit juice whereas *saft* is either the actual fruit juice without being a beverage or a kind of lemonade made of water, juice, and sugar. *Saft* is often sold as a concentrate.

190 *Prova* (to try) and *pröva* (to try) might seem like the same thing but not in all situations.

Jag prövar/provar att fråga henne. – I'll try and ask her.

---

[3] Which is one of my favorite breads.

Jag prövar/provar skorna. – I'll try the shoes.
(as a solution for something)

Får jag pröva/prova? – Can I try?

Pröva also means to test the quality of something, a solution, or to put something through a difficult test.

Jag prövar eleverna. – I'm testing the pupils.

Jag prövar lyckan. – I'm trying my luck.

Jag prövar skorna. – I'm testing/trying the shoes.
(doing quality control or using them as a solution for something, like above)

Prova is used in the sense of trying something on, like clothes. Here we can't use *pröva*.

Han provar hennes skor. – He's trying on her shoes.

Jag hatar att prova kläder. – I hate trying on clothes.

191 *Tänka*, *tycka*, and *tro* can all be translated into *to think* in English and this is where the confusion starts. This is why it's common for learners to use *tänka* as their go-to verb for this, which can either sound wrong or be confusing for the native speaker.

1. *Tänka* is used when the speaker is actually using the brain provided. It is the actual process of thinking.

Jag tänker. – I'm thinking.

2. In addition, *tänka* can sometimes be used in a way that sounds identical to *tycka* in certain contexts. However, there is a slight difference in nuance.

Jag tänker att vi ska vänta. – I'm thinking that we should wait.

Jag tycker att vi ska vänta. – I think that we should wait.

Can you spot the difference? *Tänka* is not an opinion but a more loose thread of thoughts. The speaker might be starting to form an opinion about the matter but expresses uncertainty.

192   *Tycka* means having an opinion. Easy peasy lemon squeezy.

Jag tycker att du är elak. – I think that you are mean.

193   *Tro* is something you do in church. You believe.

Jag tror på dig. – I believe in you.

Jag tror att jorden är platt. – I think that the world is flat.

194   When something is hot to the touch, or when talking about weather, *varmt* (warm) is used rather than *het* (hot).

Bastun är varm. – The sauna is hot.

Det är så varmt i dag. – It is so hot today.

Akta, det är varmt! – Careful, it's hot!

A person can however be *het* also in Swedish.

195 Some native Swedes might tell you that it's wrong to use the verb *spendera* (to spend) when talking about time, despite it being super common. They prefer the verb *tillbringa* (to spend time). *Spendera* should be reserved for money.

Now, if we look at the facts, both expressions have been around for hundreds of years. So it's safe to say that you can safely use both *spendera* and *tillbringa* when talking about time but only *spendera* when talking about money. Some *språkpoliser* ("language cops") like to be hypercorrect[4].

Hon tillbringade/spenderade sommaren hos mormor. – She spent the summer at her grandmother's.

Han spenderar sin lön på öl. – He spends his salary on beer.

Sometimes, it's even more idiomatic to just go with *vara* (to be).

Jag var hos mormor hela sommarlovet. – I spent the whole summer break at my grandma's.

196 *Små* is the plural form of the adjective *liten* (little, small). There is however a seldom used second degree form that might turn up from time to time. It turns up in expressions like *ett smärre mirakel* (a smaller miracle) and can, oddly enough, be used in both singular and plural.

▷ **151, *liten, små, lilla***

---

[4] A hypercorrection in linguistics is an error that occurs because someone thinks a certain norm applies where it really doesn't.

197 I'm sure that if you as a learner of a language come across a word like *timma* (hour), you'll be startled at first when you stumble upon the word *timme* (hour). You might have a short moment of brain fart but then shrug, think how silly you were who thought it was supposed to be *timma*, and move on with your life.

In fact both *timma* and *timme* are variants of the same word and equally correct. One originates from eastern Swedish dialects and the other from, you guessed it, western Swedish. The plural is, however, always *timmar* (even though one could think it should be *timma – timmor*).

There are other examples of this. *Trappa* and *trapp* both mean staircase. *Trapp* is considered a tad more colloquial but common enough to be important to know. *Ända* and *ände* both mean the end of an item, but only *ända* can refer to a person's behind.

198 *Gilla* (to like) and the particle verb *tycka om* (to like) are synonyms.

Jag gillar/tycker om jordgubbar. – I like strawberries.

When talking about people, however, *tycka om* can sound more affectionate or romantic.

Jag gillar dig. – I like you.
(as a person)

Jag tycker om dig. – I like you.

(And I care for you.)

199 *Handla* (to shop) and *köpa* (to buy) are often confused by learners. The difference is that *köpa* is used for individual items and refers to the exchange of money for things, whereas *handla* means to shop for a certain amount of things, most commonly groceries in everyday Swedish.

Jag måste handla. – I have to go grocery shopping.

Han behöver handla nya kläder. – He needs to shop for new clothes.

Vi ska handla mat. – We're going to buy food.

However, in some cases both words could be used depending on if you consider the item(s) to be uncountable.

Hon vill köpa godis. – She wants to buy candy.

Hon vill handla godis. – She wants to buy (shop for) candy.

Hon vill köpa kläder. – She wants to buy clothes.

Hon vill handla kläder. – She wants to buy (shop for) clothes.

Hon vill köpa mat. – She wants to buy food.

Hon vill handla mat. – She wants to buy (shop for) food.

It is thus not possible to *handla* a *klocka* (watch) or *handla* a *bok* (book), but it's fine to use the verb with *klockor* (watches) and *böcker* (books).

Jag köper en klocka. – I'm buying a watch.

Jag köper en bok. – I'm buying a book.

Jag handlar klockor. – I'm shopping for books.

Jag handlar böcker. – I'm shopping for books.

When a company or store buys stock in large volume, the particle verb *köpa in* is used instead.

200 *Sista* (the last) and *senaste* (the latest) can be tricky words to grasp since they are both often used equivalently to *last* in English.

Det senaste numret av tidningen. – The latest number of the magazine.

Det sista numret av tidningen. – The last number of the magazine.

Han har varit sjuk senaste veckan. – He's been sick for the past week.

Han var sjuk sista veckan i maj. – He was sick the last week of May.

Senaste gången vi sågs. – Last time we met.
(It might happen again.)

Sista gången vi sågs. – The last time we met.

(It won't happen again.)

To add to the confusion we also have *sist* (last time) and *senast* (last time).

Sist vi sågs. – Last time we met.

Senast vi sågs. – Last time we met.

201 *Människa, person,* and *folk* can be hard to distinguish from another and it might seem completely random to a learner which one to use.

Människa[5] literally means *human* but can also be translated as *person*. In Swedish this word is used when speaking about all people in general.

Människor har bott i skandinavien i tusentals år. – Humans have lived in Scandinavia for thousands of years.

Många människor dog i stormen. – Many people died in the storm.

Det är för många människor[6], vi går. – There are too many people, let's go.

---

[5] *Människa* is often referred back to as *hon* (she) despite not being a feminine word in modern Swedish. This also goes for clocks. There's also a tradition of referring to boats as women., which, however, has nothing to do with a historical grammatical gender.

[6] *Människor* is often made uncountable in spoken Swedish and thus *mycket människor* would work in a natural conversation.

202 *Person* means, you guessed it, *person* and is used when we pinpoint individuals.

Tolv personer dog i tågolyckan. – Twelve people died in the train crash.
(*A storm is a more spread out and thus "general" event compared to a train crash which is a much more isolated event.*)

Hur är han som person? – How is he as a person?
(*This focuses on the individual, his thoughts and mannerisms, while människa would refer to his acts as a human. Is he saving the rainforest?*)

Endast 150 personer får vistas i lokalen. – Only 150 people are allowed to be in the room.
(*Using människor here suggests that this is Noah's ark and other species would be allowed.*)

203 *Folk* can mean two things. It's either a countable word, and then means people as in an ethnic people or the citizens of a country. However, it can also be uncountable, and then it just means people in general.

det svenska folket – the Swedish people

Samerna är ett folk i norra skandinavien. – The Sami is a people in northern Scandinavia.

Det är mycket folk här idag. – There are a lot of people here today.

Vanligt folk äter tacos på fredagar. – Common people have tacos on Fridays.

Det är skillnad på folk och folk. – There is a difference between people and people.

204 *Köra* is a verb that can mean several things. Actually it's two verbs, one with a soft *k* (to drive) and one with a hard *k* (to be a backup singer). Learners often ask about *kör* (drive!) and *kör* (choir).

Jag kör till Vetlanda. – I'm driving to Vetlanda.

Han körade bakom honom i Eurovision[7] 91. – He was his backup singer in Eurovision '91.

The confusion arises when the verb *köra* (to drive) is used as *to go with* or *to do*.

Jag kör på pizza ikväll. – I'll go with pizza tonight.

Vi kör på det. – Let's go with that.

Vi kör! – Let's do it!

205 The second and third degree of *dålig* (bad), *ond* (evil), and *illa* (badly) can cause some confusion, since it depends on context as to which one is used.

A good rule of thumb for using *sämre/sämst* (worse/the worst) is to use it when the default state of things is good, neutral or expected.

Patienten blev sämre. – The patient got worse.

---

[7] Short for the *Eurovision Song Contest*.

(Since this is a patient, it's expected that something is wrong.)

Vädret är sämre idag. – The weather is worse today.
(The weather wasn't too bad yesterday.)

Du är sämre på fotboll än jag. – You're worse at soccer than me.
(Because I'm good and you're not.)

Han är sämst! – He's the worst!

206 *Värre/värst* on the other hand are used when the state was already initially bad.

Mot kvällen blev det värre. – Towards the evening it got (even) worse.

Hostan är värre i dag. – The cough is worse today.

Han blir värre när han dricker. – He gets worse when he drinks.

207 *Illa* (badly) is an adverb that can only have the second and third degree *värre/värst*. Differently from English, Swedish always uses adverbs or adverbials to describe a verb, even though they refer to your senses.

Du luktar värre nu. – You smell worse now.

Han ser värre ut idag. – He looks worse today.

Det är värre för mig. – It's worse for me.

Remember that these are only guidelines and the border

can be blurry. Languages are living things.

As a side note, *värre/värst* are often used ironically to mean the complete opposite in a sometimes sour tone.

Du ska då alltid vara värst. – You always have to outperform everyone.
(lit. "to be the worst")

Han vill alltid vara värre än alla andra. – He always wants to outperform everyone.
(lit. "to be worse than everyone else")

Det var värst! – I'll be damned!

208 One of the somewhat unique features of Swedish is the differentiation between maternal and paternal family members.

Maternal	Paternal	
mormor	farmor	grandmother
morfar	farfar	grandfather
morbror	farbror	uncle
moster	faster	aunt

209 Speaking of family members, Swedish also has a bunch of different words for different kinds of partner and family relationships.

sambo	a partner that is living under the same roof
särbo	a partner with a separate home
styvfar/styvpappa	stepfather
plastpappa	stepfather
bonuspappa	stepfather
styvmor/styvmamma	stepmother
plastmamma	stepmother
bonusmamma	stepmother
bonusfamilj	a family with a step parent

210 It can be difficult to know the difference between *pojkvän/killkompis* and *flickvän/tjejkompis* when you encounter these words.

Pojkvän and *flickvän* mean boyfriend and girlfriend – they are romantic subjects – whereas *killkompis* and *tjejkompis* mean male and female friend and are used totally platonically.

211 *Minnas* and *komma ihåg* (to remember) are synonyms but differ in one aspect: only *komma ihåg* can refer to the act of saving something in one's mind. However, both are used when we want to recall something or someone from memory.

Jag minns/<u>kommer ihåg</u> honom. – I remember him.

Jag måste <u>komma ihåg</u> att släcka ljuset. – I need to remember to blow out the candle.

212 *Glömma* and *glömma bort* (to forget) sometimes cause confusion among learners. What really is the difference?

Generally speaking there is none, however *glömma bort* could be used when something temporarily slips one's mind.

Jag glömde. – I forgot.

Jag <u>glömde bort</u>. – I forgot.

Jag glömde att det var måndag. – I forgot that it was Monday.

Jag <u>glömde bort</u> att det var måndag. – I forgot that it was Monday.

Jag glömde nycklarna. – I forgot the keys.

Jag <u>glömde bort</u> nycklarna. – I forgot about the keys.

Jag glömde boken på tåget. – I forgot the book on the train.

Jag <u>glömde bort</u> boken. – I forgot about the book.

In the last examples, *glömma bort* emphasizes the action of forgetting rather than what was forgotten. *Jag glömde bort boken på tåget* thus sounds as if the memory of a book was forgotten on a train as opposed to an actual book being left behind.

213 *Bredvid* and *jämte* both mean *beside* and are both fairly common. *Jämte* is however considered dialectal in this case.

Jag sitter bredvid/jämte henne. – I'm sitting beside her.

Sverige och Norge ligger bredvid/jämte varandra. – Sweden and Norway are located beside each other.

Jämte does however also have a standard Swedish use, which is *besides* or *together with*.

Det finns inga kvinnor jämte dig. – There are no women besides you.

Jämte Finland, Norge, Danmark och Island är Sverige ett nordiskt land. – Together with Finland, Norway, Denmark and Iceland, Sweden is a Nordic country.

214 The adjectives *långsam* (slow) and *snabb* (quick) can both be adverbs by adding the ending *-t*. They do however have the synonyms *sakta*[8] (slowly) and *fort* (quickly) that can only be adverbs – never adjectives.

Du går så sakta. – You're walking so slowly.

Karusellen snurrar för fort. – The merry-go-round is spinning

---

[8] There are a very limited few set phrases where *sakta* is an adjective: *en sakta eld* (a slow fire), *ett sakta regn* (a slow rain), etc.

too quickly.

Kom fort! – Come quickly!

215 When visiting Swedish friends during summer it could be good to know the difference between *simma* (to swim) and *bada* (to bathe).

Now *bada* doesn't necessarily mean that we're going to wash ourselves. It also means *to almost completely submerge one's body into water*. So if you're just going to cool down in the nearby lake, you're most likely going to use this word. Asking or being asked to go and *simma*, is a specific question about transporting yourself in water with arms and legs.

And by the way, don't confuse *simma* with *svimma* (to faint).

216 *Antingen ... eller* (either ... or), *varken ... eller* (neither ... nor), and *vare sig ... eller* (neither ... nor) could be hard to wrap your head around. They work slightly differently.

When listing two alternatives, *antingen eller* is the one we use.

Antingen går du hem **eller** så stannar du kvar. – You'll either go home or stay.

It can also be used to express that there are two options but they don't matter. This is slightly informal.

Du måste gå **antingen** du vill **eller** inte. – You have to go whether you want to or not.

217 *Varken eller* and *vare sig eller* are both used in negated sentences. The difference here is that the negation is inferred when *varken eller* is used.

Han ville **varken** stanna **eller** gå hem. – He neither wanted to stay nor go home.

Han ville **inte vare sig** stanna **eller** gå hem. – He neither wanted to stay nor go home.

This rule is starting to disintegrate so that both expressions are interchangeable, with or without a negation. No one would probably bat an eye.

Both can be used to express two potential options that don't matter.

Du måste gå **vare sig** du vill det **eller** inte. – You have to go whether you want to or not.

Du måste gå **varken** du vill det **eller** inte. – You have to go whether you want to or not.

218 A word that is very difficult to explain to learners is *trivas*. This deponent verb expresses the feeling of being content and comfortable. It is often translated as *to like it somewhere* or *to be happy with something*.

Trivs du i Sverige? – Do you like it in Sweden?

Han trivs på nya jobbet. – He likes his new job.

Hon trivs med valet. – She's content with her choice.

De trivs inte i skolan. – They don't feel happy being in school.

219 *Passa på* (to seize the opportunity) is one of those ultimate Swedish expressions that never seem to have received any fame but capture the essence of Swedish culture.

Most of the year is cold and rainy, so when the weather invites you to go on a hike, you have to *passa på*. This mindset is also applied to other situations resulting in the phrase being used a lot, with or without an object. The expression is often used together with *måste* or *få* (to have to), which says even more about this phenomenon. You always have to seize the opportunity.

Vi måste passa på att gå ut. – We have to seize the opportunity and go out.

Man får ju passa på när det bjuds. – One has to seize the opportunity when being treated.

Passa på nu när det är gratis. – Seize the opportunity now when it's free.

Ja, man måste ju passa på. – Yeah, one has to seize the opportunity.

Fråga henne! Passa på nu medan hon är på gott humör. – Ask her! Seize the opportunity now while she's in a good mood.

Jag passar på och äter nu när barnen sover. – I'm going to

seize the opportunity to eat now while the children are asleep.

220 *Duktig* is somewhat hard to translate, but it's a widely used word that learners usually snap up. The problem is that it can have certain condescending connotations, which the learner isn't aware of, making it sound comedic or rude at times.

Duktig is essentially used when someone is skilled.

Han är duktig på att måla. – He's skilled at painting.

Hon är duktig på att sjunga. – She's skilled at singing.

De är duktiga musiker. – They are skilled musicians.

Du är så duktig på svenska. – You're so good at Swedish.

However, when using it stand-alone or with words that aren't really skills, it rather means *well-behaved* or *good*. This is something you'd rather say to a child. Using it with adults doing mundane things can sound very condescending and the word should be used with caution. **Don't use it as a translation for a job well done with grownups.**

Hon är en duktig flicka. – She's a good girl.

Vad du är duktig, gubben. – Well done, buddy!

Det var duktigt. – Well done.

Du måste alltid vara så himla duktig hela tiden. – You always need to be so good all the time.

It can also be used as an intensifier.

Nu är man duktigt trött! – Now one is really tired.

221 One of the most exciting aspects of foreign languages is the possibility of stumbling upon words that don't exist in your native language. Swedish is no exception and several words have no direct equivalent in English.

gapa	to open one's mouth
blunda	to close one's eyes
panta	to return cans and bottles for a deposit
hinna	to make it in time
orka	to feel like/have the energy for something
snusa	to use snus[9]
vaska	to pour out expensive drinks into the sink to show one's wealth
slippa	to not have to do something

222 Some words might not exist in other countries since they are so specific to Sweden and Swedish culture. They can be based

---

[9] A tobacco product placed under the lip.

on laws, names for institutions or different product names, but they could also be words that only refer to Nordic or Scandinavian occurrences.

älv (river)	Only used with rivers existing in the Nordic countries.
fjäll (mountain, mountain area)	Mountain above the treeline, usually only used with mountains in the Nordic countries.
riksdagen (Sweden's parliament)	Commonly used with the parliaments of the Nordic countries as well. The word *parlament* also exists on a more general level.
Systembolaget (liquor store)	Sweden's state owned alcohol monopoly. Anything about 3.5 vol% is sold here. Usually referred to as *systemet* or *bolaget*.
hemtjänst (home care)	Home care provided by municipalities. Often referred to in its definite form *hemtjänsten*.
vabba (to tend to a sick child)	VAB is an abbreviation for *vård av barn* (care for child) which is a shorter

name of a law that makes it possible to stay home from work and receive compensation when one's child is sick.

vobba (to work at home when one's child is home sick)

This verb is a combination of *jobba* (to work) and *vabba*.

Posten (the mail)

The Swedish postal service, now often referred to as *Postnord* after a merger with the Danish postal service.

vårdcentral (care central)

A clinic for non-emergencies run by Sweden's regions, where people can see a doctor. Often referred to in the definite form *vårdcentralen*.

vårt avlånga land (our oblong country)

Sweden is oblong and is therefore often referred to as *our oblong country*.

bankomat (ATM)

A joint venture between several Swedish banks. A more neutral word would be *uttagsautomat*.

Skatteverket (the tax

Sweden's tax authority,

authority)

which also takes care of citizen registration.

FAQ & Common Pitfalls

223 A very common error for native English speakers and often for people who learned English as their first foreign language is putting the verb in the wrong place.

Swedish uses the so-called V2 word order which states that the verb has to come in second place. This is normal for Germanic languages and English is the exception here. This is most prominent when initiating a sentence with an adverbial.

Förra sommaren åt jag jordgubbar. – Last summer I ate strawberries.

Förra sommaren (last summer) is an adverbial and both words belong together as a phrase and the first element of this sentence. *Åt* (ate) is the verb – or predicate, since we're talking about constituents – and goes in second place.

This is one of the most, if not the most, prominent errors when people speak Swedish as a foreign language.

224 When learners introduce themselves, they tend to use adjectives to refer to their ethnicity or country of origin. It's more idiomatic to go with a noun instead!

Jag är amerikan. – I'm an American.

Jag är österrikare. – I'm an Austrian.

Adjectives are used as attributes or reserved for anything that isn't a person.

Vasen är japansk. – The vase is Japanese.

Jag har köpt en svensk bil. – I've bought a Swedish car.

225 The different words meaning *because* are often asked about within my community and that totally makes sense. Swedish has several words that cannot be used exactly the same, which is obviously super confusing.

Eftersom is the first word that comes to mind when translating *because*. It's used in the same cases and can be considered neutral in style.

Jag är arg **eftersom** du är elak. – I'm angry because you're being mean.

226 Another one is *därför (att)*. It has the same status as *eftersom* but there's a but: you **can not** use *därför att* when the subordinate clause stands in front of the main clause. It needs to connect the sentences directly. In this case we use *eftersom* instead.

Jag är arg **därför att** du är elak. – I'm angry because you're being mean.

Eftersom du är elak är jag arg. – Because you're being mean, I'm angry.

It can however be used to answer a question, like its siblings:

– Varför städar du huset? (Why are you cleaning the house?)
– Eftersom/Därför att vi får gäster senare. (Because we're having guests over later.)

It can also – without *att* – act as an annoyed stand-alone answer to *varför* (why) when a proper answer is being avoided.

– Varför gjorde du så? (Why did you do that?)
– Därför! (Because!)

In this regard, it's also used the same as *that's why* to conclude an explanation.

Och därför har vi inte gjort det än. – And that's why we haven't done it yet.

227 *För att* is a causal expression but very common in spoken Swedish. It often comes together with *bara* (only).

Jag är arg **för att** du är elak. – I'm angry because you're being mean.

Bara för att du är arg behöver du inte vara elak. – Just because you're angry you don't need to be mean.

För att can also mean *in order to*:

För att tända en brasa behöver man trä[1]. – In order to light a fire one needs wood.

---

[1] *Träd* means tree. *Trä* means wood.

228 *För* is a **conjunction** which means that it connects a **main clause with a main clause** with a meaning closer to the English word *for*. Colloquially it can act as a **subjunction**, though, like all the others.

Jag är arg **för** du är elak. – I'm angry because you're being mean.

This is most evident in negated sentences, where *inte* (not) would shift places in a subordinate clause.

För han är inte här. – For he's not here.
(conjunction)

Eftersom han inte är här. – Because he's not here.

För han inte är här. – Because he's not here.
(subjunction)

För can't – similarly to *därför att* – initiate a subordinate clause resolving into a main clause. But can act as an answer to a question.

▷ **226, *därför att***

– Varför städar du huset? (Why are you cleaning the house?)
– För vi får gäster senare. (Because we're having guests over later.)

229 *För* **is not the general translation for the English word *for*.** There are three prepositions to use in different situations: *till*, *åt*, and *för*.

För is used with verbs that transfer information or a performance of some sort.

Jag sjunger för dig. – I'll sing for you.

Han berättar en saga för sin dotter. – He's telling his daughter a story.

Hon förklarade det för henne. – She explained it to her.

230 *Till* (to) is used in the most tangible way when it's used for direction.

Vi åker till Sverige. – We're going to Sweden.

However it's used when there's a receiving end of an item.

Jag har något till dig. – I have something for you.

Jag bakar till mötet. – I'm baking for the meeting.

Hon köper en present till honom. – She's buying a gift for him.

231 *Åt* (towards) is also used for direction but the context doesn't reveal if the destination is even going to be reached.

Vi går åt det hållet. – We'll go in that direction.

Åt is otherwise similar in use to *till* but often stresses that the action is done in someone's stead or as a favor.

Jag har något åt dig. – I have something for you.

Jag bakar åt dig. – I'm baking for you.
(Either something for you, as a favor, or on your behalf.)

Hon köper en present åt honom. – She's buying a gift for him.
(The gift is either for him or bought on his behalf, depending on the context.)

232   There is sometimes this misconception that the greeting *hej* would be too casual because of the similarity to English *hey*. This is not the case.

Hej is the basic go-to greeting that works in all situations. In this regard *hallå* is actually the casual one when used like this.

The standard use of *hallå* is as a question and call for attention or as a signal for answering the phone. In this case, it's equivalent to *hello*.

233   Besides *hej* and *hallå*, there are numerous, more or less, colloquial ways to greet someone. Since Swedes are pretty casual, most of them can be used with anyone. I've tried to place them on a scale so that you can choose the one you feel the most content with.

god dag (good day)	formal
god förmiddag (good before-noon)	formal
god middag (good noon)	formal

god eftermiddag (good afternoon)	formal
god kväll (good evening)	formal
god afton (good evening)	formal, dated
god natt (good night)	neutral
god morgon (good morning)	neutral
hej på dig[2]	semi-neutral
hejsan	semi-neutral
tjenare	colloquial
tjena	colloquial
tja	colloquial
tjenixen	colloquial
halloj	colloquial

234 One of the seven deadly sins is to write a compound word as two words. This sometimes changes the pronunciation but it might also change the meaning.

Regard this classic example:

en brun hårig sköterska – a brown hairy nurse

---

[2] This one could make you sound surprised.

en brunhårig sköterska – a brown-haired nurse

235 Learners usually have a problem understanding exactly how to use the verb *må* (to feel). This third conjugation group verb expresses one's feeling in terms of physical health. It can only stand together with positive or negative adverbs.

Jag mår bra. – I feel fine.

Jag mår dåligt. – I don't feel good.

Jag mår utmärkt. – I feel excellent.

Jag mår uselt. – I feel terrible.

In this case, it's not possible to use *vara* (to be): ~~Jag är bra (I'm good)~~.

In the same manner, it's not possible to use *må* with feelings, which is also a common mistake. In this case we use *vara* (to be) or *känna sig* (to feel).

Jag är trött. – I'm tired.

Jag känner mig trött. – I feel tired.

~~Jag mår trött. – I feel tired.~~

236 *Båda* and *både* might seem like the same word but do in fact mean different things. *Både* is the first part of the two word adverb *både och* (either or). This is confusing because it can be translated as *both* when it's not separated. Let me demonstrate.

Jag gillar både tårta och glass. – I like both cake and ice cream.

Jag gillar både och. – I like both.

However, *båda* just means *both*, like so:

Båda tårtorna hade grädde. – Both cakes had cream.

Jag gillar båda (två). – I like both.

In the case of the last sentence, *båda* is mostly followed by *två* (two).

There is also the word *bägge* which has its origin in the possessive case of *båda*. In contemporary Swedish it's a synonym that might be considered slightly casual.

Jag gillar bägge. – I like both.

237 Another question that pops up a lot is what is the real difference between *god* and *bra*. Understandable, since *god* is clearly related to *good*. But then there's *bra*, which doesn't look like *good* at all, and makes everyone giggle like pubertal teenagers, but supposedly means *good*.

Here's the deal. *Bra* came into the language from Low German *brav* (well-behaved, honest, good) in the 17th century. Today, it's the default when talking about someone being good at something or something being done well (yes, it also means *well*). It's also used when someone has recovered from an illness or as an intensifier.

Jag är bra på matte. – I'm good at math.

Det är bra! – That's good!

Hon sjunger bra. – She sings well.

Jag mår bra. – I feel good.

Han är bra igen. – He has recovered.

Det tog ett bra tag. – It took a good while.

God[3] is used when talking about someone's or something's good qualities, as the opposite to evil, as an intensifier, but foremost to describe sensory input like flavor and fragrance (in which case the comparative forms are *godare, godast*[4]).

Hon avslutar dagen med en god bok. – She ends her day with a good book.

Jag kommer med goda nyheter. – I'm coming with good news.

Han är en riktigt god vän. – He's a really good friend.

Hon är alltigenom god. – She is good through and through.

De väntade en god stund. – They waited a good while.

Det luktar gott här. – It smells good here.

---

[3] Hallelujah!

[4] Yes, *gooder* and *the goodest*.

Maten smakar gott. – The food tastes good.

238 When introducing yourself or someone else, Swedes use the verb *heta* (to be named). It is very common for learners to use *vara* (to be) here because it's how you say it in English. This is, however, not idiomatic in Swedish.

Jag heter Sven. – I'm Sven/My name is Sven.

There is one case though where *vara* is used like this, and it's when emphasizing who someone is.

Det är jag som är Lars. – (lit.) It's me who am Lars.

239 *Mena* (to mean) is often used by learners in place of *betyda* (to mean). The difference is that *betyda* should be used when something has a meaning, whereas *mena* is used when the subject is actively expressing something. It is perhaps more easily explained with *to be saying*.

Vad menar du? – What do you mean/What are you saying?

Vad betyder det? – What does it mean?

"Book" betyder bok på engelska. – "Book" means book in English.

Han menar att du är dum. – He's saying that you're stupid.

Inanimate objects can't really be the subject of *mena* but they can still have a meaning.

Du betyder allt för mig. – You mean everything to me.

Den här låten betyder allt. – This song means everything.

240 It's common for people to use the verb *känna* just like *to know* in English. It's a verb that can both mean *to feel* and *to know a person*.

Jag känner att det blir bra. – I feel that it's going to be good.

Jag känner hans mamma. – I know his mother.

However, learners frequently use this also when talking about something or someone they only know about, which can cause confusion. Instead we need the particle verb *känna till* for this.

Jag <u>känner till</u> Sverige. – I know (about) Sweden.

Jag <u>känner till</u> honom. – I know (about) him.

Using only *känna* sounds like the person talked about is a personal friend.

An additional way to express that something is known is with the phrase *höra talas om* (to hear about).

Jag har hört talas om honom. – I've heard about him.

241 In Swedish, as opposed to English, centuries aren't talked about in ordinal numbers but are referred to by the actual year.

1800-talet /aaaartonhundra-taaaalet/ – the 19th century

1900-talet /nittttonhundra-taaaalet/ – the 20th century

2000-talet /tjuuuugohundra-taaaalet/ – the 21th century
(also referred to as tvåtusentalet)

242   Using a preposition together with the name of a language doesn't work the same way as in English. The phrase *in Swedish* is often directly translated as *i svenska* by learners. The correct preposition for this is, however, *på svenska* (surprise, surprise).

Vad heter det på svenska? – What is it called in Swedish?

Kan du säga det på svenska? – Can you say it in Swedish?

Sometimes learners also tend to say something like *tala på svenska* (speak in Swedish) which would be wrong also in English.

Jag talar svenska. – I speak Swedish.
(No preposition, just like in English.)

The preposition *i* can be used with **the definite form of the language** when talking about features of Swedish or glossary.

Ordet existerar inte i svenskan. – The word doesn't exist in Swedish.

I svenskan finns inget ackusativ. – In Swedish there is no accusative.

Tips, Fun Facts & Good-To-Knows

243 Good news! If you need to create your own verbs, you could just take any words (perhaps a noun or why not an English verb), add the ending *-a* and treat it as a verb in the first conjugation group. This is great if you don't want to ruin the flow of your conversation as a learner.

▷ 20, the first conjugation group

244 If you need a noun, but you only know the corresponding verb, you can nounify it with the prefixes *-ande*, *-ning*, or *-ing* (used when the stem already ends on *-n* or when it ends on a consonant + *-n*, *-l*, or *-r*).

It might sound too formal, or just wrong, but people will (hopefully) know what you're trying to say without you ruining your flow. There might, of course, already be words with these endings, like *spelande* (gambling) and *spelning* (concert).

The ending *-ande* makes the word into the present participle which can act as an *ett* word. It is often used when describing the act as ongoing and annoying.

Vilket himla solande! – What a lot of sunning going on!

245 The *-is* suffix creates nicknames and slang words. It is originally a kind of pseudo-Latin that began to emerge in the 1800s. The *en* words construct the plural on *-ar* and the *ett* words lack a plural ending, as we know. This can basically be seen as an unofficial Swedish diminutive which is used to express affection, endearment or just to shorten words.

1. Some words stand with one foot in slang land and with one in the standard language or are old enough to be a stable, yet colloquial, occurrance in the language.

grattis	congrats
godis	candy
bästis	bestie
kändis	celeb
hemlis	secret
kompis	buddy
dagis[1]	kindergarten
loppis	flea market
kondis	bakery
brådis	urgent, in a hurry

---

[1] Since the *daghem* (daycare) institution was changed in the late 1990s to *förskola* (pre-school), the term is starting to become obsolete and replaced with *föris*. This is taking a long, long time though.

trummis	drummer
skådis	actor
skummis	suspicious person
mjukis	softie
alkis	alcoholic
fegis	fearful person
folkis[2]	beer
skräckis	horror movie
tjockis	fat person
chaffis	chauffeur
fjortis	obnoxious, mostly girly, teenager
målis	goalkeeper
poppis	popular
mellis	snack
lantis	hillbilly
osis	bad luck

---

[2] *Folköl* is a Swedish definition of beer most commonly at 3.5 vol%, allowed to be sold at the grocery store as opposed to stronger beverages which have to be sold at *Systembolaget*.

champis	champagne
knäppis	silly person
sotis	jealous
bergis	very sure
bombis	very sure
fräckis	dirty joke
bundis	befriended

2. Other words are a lot newer or sporadically created and can sound comical or affectionate depending on the context.

sötis	cutie
gosis	cuddly person

3. Abbreviations for places and institutions are sometimes constructed with the -is ending.

Mallis	Mallorca
Medis	Medborgarplatsen
Rålis	Rålambshovsparken
Bagis	Bagarmossen
Teknis	Kungl. tekniska högskolan

(Royal technical institute)

246 Similar to the Swedish pseudo-latin ending *-is*, there's the ending *-o* to create colloquial variants of short words. This is often used for pejoratives.

▷ **245, fake diminutive with *-is***

fetto	fatso
pervo	pervert
pucko	stupid
miffo	freak

There are some positive words but they are often (but not exclusively) used sarcastically.

snyggo	handsome person
hygglo	kind person
lyllo	lucky person

Generally these words are nouns but there are examples where they can be adjectives as well.

pretto	pretentious, pretentious

	snob
värdo	worthless
mysko	weird, peculiar

247 In Swedish we use the letter *é* in some words to mark a stressed long vowel in some words, mostly French loans. It can sometimes be spotted in last names as well.

idé	idea
kafé	cafe
armé	army
succé	success
diarré	diarrhea
gonorré	gonorrhea

248 Opposites (as well as pejoratives) are generally constructed with the prefix *o-* (un-) in Swedish.

trolig (believable)	otrolig (unbelievable)
ansvarig (responsible)	oansvarig (irresponsible)
behaglig (pleasant)	obehaglig (unpleasant)
vän (friend)	ovän (enemy[3])

djur (animal)	odjur (beast)
ljud (sound)	oljud (noise, jangle)
tålig (patient, tough)	otålig (impatient)

Just as a tiny sidenote, the word *obra* (bad) is a colloquial and mostly (but not always) a kind of comedic or ironic word. You might hear it if you're lucky.

A bigger and more important parenthesis is the word *orolig* that means *worried*. This is the original opposite of *rolig* (calm) which in Danish and Norwegian still has this meaning. **Rolig, however (a huge however), means *funny* in modern Swedish.**

249 Despite having this awesome way to create opposites with one single prefix, most words have completely different words as their opposite counterparts.

bra (good)	dålig (bad)
ljus (light)	mörk (dark)
lång (long)	kort (short)
hög (high)	låg (low)
fin (pretty)	ful (ugly)

---

[3] *Fiende* is the actual word for *enemy*, whereas *ovän* just means that two people are on bad terms.

snäll (kind)	elak (mean)
smart (smart)	dum (dumb)
lugn (calm)	orolig (restless)
glad (happy)	ledsen (sad), arg (angry)
modig (courageous)	feg (cowardly)

250 A nominal phrase (a phrase that acts as one entity in a clause) gets the possessive -*s* at the end.

De svenska flickornas ögon. – The Swedish girls' eyes.

When talking about two separate entities, giving both nouns the suffix emphasizes their individuality.

Svenskars och finländares historia. – The history of Swedes and Finlanders.
(Emphasis is on their individual history.)

Svenskar och finländares historia – The history of Swedes and Finlanders.
(Emphasis is on their common history.)

251 The usage of *to do* as a helper verb in English is rather unfamiliar to Swedes but actually exists in other Germanic languages in different constellations.

In Swedish we can use a similar construction with the verb *göra* (to do) as a placeholder when stressing the action requires the main verb to act as the first element in a sentence.

Because of the so-called V2 word order, another verb has to come in second place.

Äter kakor gör jag varje dag. – Eating cookies I do every day.
(The first element here is the phrase äter kakor.)

Göra is also used as a placeholder to point back to something and to avoid repetition.

– Gillar du mig? (Do you like me?)
– Ja, det gör jag. (Yes, I do.)

Ingen tror att jag gillar fotboll men det gör jag. – No one thinks that I like soccer but I do.

252 When talking about people in quantity, it is common to omit that actual word.
▷ **201, *människa, person, folk***

Många kom på festen. – Many (people) came to the party.

Bara några få var i kyrkan. – Only a few (people) were in the church.

De flesta var nöjda. – Most (people) were satisfied.

253 There are numerous ways to say *yes* and *no* in Swedish, some of which are more colloquial than others.

ja (yes)	neutral
ja visst (yes of course)	neutral

ja så klart (yes of course)	neutral
absolut (absolutely)	neutral
naturligtvis (of course)	neutral
jo	colloquial
japp	colloquial
jajamänsan	colloquial
jajjemen	colloquial
yes	colloquial
yesbox	colloquial
shhhhhhhhhp (famous northern Swedish inhaling sound)	colloquial

The ways to say *no* directly are limited (it's just too direct for a confrontation-avoiding Swede), however there are expressions that don't seem to mean *no*, that really mean *no*: *nja* (yes and no), *kanske* (maybe), *jag vet inte* (I don't know), *jag tror inte det* (I don't think so), *jag är inte säker* (I'm not sure).

254 Swedes exclaim *oj* (oops) or *nämen*[4] (wow) when they are surprised but also use these words in variations in a bunch of situations.

---

[4] Really *nej men*.

Oj, förlåt! – Oops, sorry!
(A Swede bumped into someone.)

Oj, då. /ooooj då/ – Oh.
(A Swede heard some bad news.)

Oj! – Oops!
(A Swede just dropped a plate.)

Oj! – Oh, crap!
(A Swede just realized something, what could it be?)

Oj! /Ooooj/ – Wow!
(A Swede just saw an albino moose.)

Oj, oj, oj! /ojoj-OJ/ – Look at that!
*(A Swede saw northern lights **and** an albino moose at the same time.)*

Ojojoj /oooojooooojooooojooooj/ – Poor thing
(A Swede is comforting a child.)

Ojojoj! – Careful!
(A Swede saw a child juggling knives.)

Oj, oj, oj... – Ouch, ouch, ouch...
(A Swede is an old man, whose intervertebral disc hurts.)

Nämen! – Well hello there!
(A Swede met an old friend.)

Nämen! – What are you doing?
(A Swede just saw a child picking their nose.)

Nämen (oj)! – Oops!

(A Swede knocked over a glass.)

Nämen! – What, really?
(A Swede just heard that a friend is getting married.)

Nämen! /näMENNNN/ – Wow!
(A Swede just got a cool gift.)

Nämen! – What a distasteful suggestion!
(A Swede just got asked to do naughty things.)

Nämen... /NÄÄÄÄmen/ – Hmm...
(A Swede just got something to think about.)

Nämen... /NÄÄÄÄmen/ – Well...
(A Swede is searching for words.)

Nämen... /NÄÄÄÄmen/ – So, anyway...
(A Swede wants to end the conversation.)

**As you can see, there's lots of variation and this is
something you'll have to learn with practice.**

255 A tip to sound more natural in Swedish is to stop using
mycket (much) all too much as an intensifier in spoken and
casual Swedish. It is far more common in contemporary
Swedish to say *väldigt* (giantly) or use the prefix *jätte-* (giant).

Hon är väldigt arg. – She's really angry.

Mamma blev jättearg. – Mom got really angry.

256 Some verbs only have partial conjugation just like the
adjectives we talked about earlier.

▷ 149, defective adjectives

Varda (to become) is used only in its past tense form (*vart*) in contemporary Swedish. This is considered regional spoken Swedish but its use is rather widely spread.

Måste (to have to/must) is generally only used in the present tense and past tense. Since these forms look the same, the past tense is often replaced with *var tvungen*.

Skola is used in a bunch of situations but could generally be translated as *will* (future tense). You will only really see this in the present tense (*ska*) and the past tense (*skulle*) in contemporary Swedish.

257 Using the present tense to express a future action along with a personal pronoun can turn into a demand.

Nu städar du ditt rum. – You will clean your room now.

Nu går du och lägger dig. – You will go to bed now.
▷ 28, the future tense

258 Since Swedish has several ways of constructing the passive voice, it could be tricky to know which ones to choose. Using passive with the ending -*s* is often prefered (because, as always, these are loose guidelines) in the following cases:

1. Verbs used for expressing thought or storytelling like *säga* (to say), *påstå* (to claim), *tro* (to believe), *se* (to see), and *höra* (to hear), tend to prefer the passive with -*s*.

Han sägs bo på en hemlig ö. – He's said to be living on a secret island.

Hon tros vara en ängel. – She's believed to be an angel.

De påstås ha mördat statsministern. – They are alleged to have murdered the Prime Minister.

2. The passive voice with *-s* is also commonly used when the subject is the general *det* (it).
▷ **127, the general *det***

Det äts och dricks på festen. – People are eating and drinking at the party.

Det sägs att trollen tog honom. – It's being said that the trolls took him.

Det görs inte så lätt. – It can't be done that easily.

3. When a helper verb is a part of the passive phrase, passive with *-s* is prefered.

Häxan måste brännas. – The witch has to be burned.

Det ska tackas och bockas när man hälsar. – One must thank and bow when greeting someone.

Biljetten måste köpas innan konserten. – The ticket has to be purchased before the concert.

4. When the active verb usually takes an object.

Finsk tango dansades på Finlandsbåten. – Finnish tango was

danced on the cruise to Finland.

Boken läses bäst i en hängmatta. – The book is best read in a hammock.

Maten äts vid bordet. – The food is eaten at the table.

5. When a state is expressed as being the general norm.

Huset bebos av skator. – The house is being inhabited by magpies.

Alkohol köps på Systembolaget[5]. – Alcohol is bought at Systembolaget.

Filmen visas på bio. – The movie is being shown at the cinema.

6. Requests and indirect orders.
▷ **179, formal requests with *vänligen***

Kläderna slängs i containern. – The clothes are to be thrown into the container.

Sängarna bäddas varje morgon. – The beds are to be made every morning.

Resenärer ombes att ha passen redo. – Travelers are asked to have their passports ready.

Rummen lämnas före klockan 12. – The rooms are to be left

---

[5] Sweden has an alcohol monopoly which means that strong drinks are only sold at *Systembolaget*.

before 12 o'clock.

259   The passive voice can also be constructed with the helper verb *bli* (to become) + past participle, similar to *to get* in English. There are of course certain tendencies that show where the *bli* passive is prefered.

1. *Bli* is more often used with people and animals.

Hon gillar att bli kramad. – She likes to be hugged.

Hunden blir jagad av katten. – The dog is getting chased by the cat.

2. When the action has a clear result.

Han blev klippt hos frisören. – He got a new haircut at the hairdresser.
(lit. "He got cut at the hairdresser.")

Huset blev färdigmålat i lördags. – The house was completely painted last Saturday.

3. The *bli* passive can be used in the present tense to indicate the future.

Tårtan blir inte äten om ni kommer för sent. – The cake won't get eaten if you arrive too late.

Utan hjälp blir flaggstången inte rest. – Without help the flag pole won't be risen.

4. It can also express a guarantee for something to happen.

Du blir körd till tandläkaren imorgon. – You're going to get a ride to the dentist tomorrow.

5. When the subject can somehow influence whether or not something will happen due to avoiding or engaging in certain situations.

De blev rånade på alla pengar. – They got robbed of all their money.

Han blev blöt av regnet. – He got wet by the rain.

Hon blev sparkad av en kamel. – She was kicked by a camel.

6. The passive voice with -s is avoided when there is a deponent verb present to avoid obvious confusion that would arise when the passive voice looks like a deponent verb. Compare the following examples:

Jag retas. – I'm teasing.

Jag blir retad. – I'm getting teased.

Han nyps. – He's pinching.

Han blir nypt. – He's getting pinched.

7. To avoid repetition, bli is used when another verb is already in the passive voice with -s.

Han sågs bli buren. – He was seen getting carried.

Hon påstås bli avskedad imorgon. – She's claimed to get fired tomorrow.

260 The present participle can also get an *-s* in spoken Swedish when describing an ongoing action, just like the English *-ing* form.

Han gick på gatan ätandes på en köttbulle. – He was walking on the street, eating a meatball.

Be aware that particle verbs are fused together with the particle as a prefix in the past participle.

▷ **38, particle verbs**

en överkörd man – a run-over man
(from köra över)

261 In Swedish we often omit the possessive pronoun with some verbs where it's obvious that we're talking about the subject's own things, mostly body parts. Here we use the definite form of the noun instead.

Jag tvättar händerna. – I'm washing my hands.

Jag har ont i benet. – My leg hurts.

262 Filler words aren't always only meaningless bulk in a sentence. In Swedish there are several that convey a bunch of information that would need several words to translate into English.

Ju is used to provide some known information. It roughly

translates to "as you know".

Jag är ju svensk. – I'm Swedish, as you know.

Jag är ju svensk! – But I'm Swedish!
(Don't you know, can't you see.)

It can also express that the speaker is surprised about the situation. Frequently used sarcastically.

Det var ju bra! – How nice/good!

Det var ju gott! – This is delicious!

263 *Nog* is used to convey a piece of information that the speaker assumes to be true.

Jag är nog för dum. – I'm probably too stupid.

264 *Väl* is another word, used when expressing an assumption or when seeking affirmation. Basically corresponds to a question tag in English.

Jag är väl snäll? – I'm nice, don't you think?

Han är väl polis? – He's a police officer, isn't he?

Bordet är väl för stort. – I guess the table is too big.

265 Talking about question tags, *eller hur* is the oh so glorious one.

Du är hans mamma, eller hur? – You're his mom, aren't you?

Jag är bäst, eller hur? – I'm the best, amirite?

Eller hur can also be used colloquially as a way to agree with the recent statement:

– Han är så snygg! (He's so hot!)
– Eller hur! (I know, right?!)

266 *Va*, with a short *a* sound, comes from *vad* (what) and is also a very common question tag.

Du är hans mamma, va? – You're his mom, aren't you?

267 *Eller* is another one, paired with sentences that are already questions, it's used to seek confirmation.

Får jag komma in eller? – May I come in?

It can also be translated with *or something* in more aggressive rhetorical questions.

Är du dum eller? – Are you stupid or something?

268 It's often taught that Swedish doesn't have a present continuous tense. It's however possible to express ongoing actions in other ways.

1. Adding *just nu* (right now) to the sentence, will indicate that it's happening – drumroll – right now.

Han diskar just nu. – He's doing the dishes (right now).

Hon talar i telefon just nu. – She's on the phone (right now).

De äter just nu. – They're eating (right now).

2. The particle verb *hålla på* emphasizes that an action is being performed in the now.
▷ **38, particle verbs**

Jag håller på att städa. – I'm cleaning.

Håll inte på! – Stop it!

Vad håller du på med? – What are you up to?

3. *Stå* (to stand), *ligga* (to lie), *sitta* (to sit) paired with another verb is a common tool to express that the action is happening right now.
▷ **138, *stå, ligga, sitta***

Han ligger och sover. – He's sleeping
(lit. "He's lying down and sleeping.")

Jag står och lagar mat. – I'm making food.
(lit. "I'm standing and making food.")

Hon sitter och läser. – She's reading.
(lit. "She's sitting down and reading.")

The position in which something is happening is important and has to correspond to the context. It's not possible to just take any of these verbs to construct "the present continuous".

Similarly, it's also possible to use additional verbs that indicate a position/state in which the subject is in, like *hänga* (to hang) or *gå* (to walk).

Här hänger du och sover. – Here you're hanging and sleeping.

Flickan går och sjunger. – Girl is walking and singing.

4. The passive voice or verbs in the active voice standing as deponents, create a feeling of something ongoing.
▷ **35, deponent verbs**

De pussas. – They are kissing.

De kramas. – They are hugging.

Det lagas mat här ser jag! – I see you're cooking!

5. Present participle expresses that something is done right now in the present.

Han gick ätande på en köttbulle. – He was walking while eating a meatball.

This only works with another main verb, expressing that something is done at the same time as something else, and does not exactly correspond to the English present continuous with *to be*.

269 Constructions like *you idiot* are formed with the possessive pronoun in Swedish rather than the subject pronoun.

Din idiot! – You idiot!

Era idioter! – You idiots!

270 Bursting out in a *how* + adjective/adverb is done with the word *vad* (what) instead of *hur* (how).

Vad kul! – How fun!

Vad tråkigt! – How sad!

Vad trevligt! – How nice!

271 A tip for constructing sentences in Swedish is to pay attention to the verbs. Swedish[6] relies heavily on the use of those and it's important to check if there is already one single verb that can express what you want to say.

Even if you could use a noun, conveying the same thing with a verb might sound more idiomatic.

Blunda! – Close your eyes!
(Rather than stäng ögonen.)

Han heter Olle. – His name is Olle.

De ska skiljas. – They're filing for divorce.

Hon cyklar. – She's riding her bike.

272 *Alltså*, *liksom*, and *ba* are common fillers in spoken Swedish. **Don't overuse them.**

Alltså (thus), when used as a casual filler, is used to mark

---

[6] As opposed to Finland-Swedish which, due to its Finnish influences, relies more on nouns than verbs.

annoyance, to show that something should be known, to initiate a sentence, or to put emphasis on the sentence. It's pronounced, and commonly written, *asså* which shows that it has basically become its own word and has little to do with the original *alltså*.

Asså! – (The speaker is clearly annoyed.)

Asså, kan du hjälpa mig? – Hey, can you help me?

Han är så jävla snygg, asså! – He's so damn hot!

Asså du kan inte gå dit. – Uhm, you can't go there.

273 *Liksom* (like) is, like, used, like, the English filler like.

Han liksom försökte liksom kyssa mig liksom. – He like tried to like kiss me.

274 *Ba* comes from *bara* (only) and is used like the English filler *just like* and is often used as a tool in story telling to indicate indirect speech.

Han ba försökte ba kyssa mig ba. – He just like tried to just like kiss me.

Han ba: "Det är slut." – He was just like: "It's over."

These fillers are super common but luckily seldom as extreme as in these examples. Use them, but use them with some grace.

275 In colloquial Swedish, *en annan* (someone else, another) is sometimes used to refer to the first person singular. You know. Just check the example.

▷ **153, annan, andra, till**

En annan måste ju jobba hela helgen. – I myself have to work the whole weekend.

276 *Till* (until, for), *medan* (while), *förrän* (before) and *tillbaka* (back) are words that have casual forms with an added trailing -*s*: *tills*[7], *medans*, *förräns*, *tillbaks*. These forms are very common in spoken Swedish and casual texts.

Vi behöver chips till/tills imorgon. – We need chips for tomorrow.

Han såg på tv medan/medans han åt. – He was watching TV while he ate.

Vi ses inte förrän/förräns[8] ikväll. – We won't see each other until tonight.

Jag är snart tillbaka/tillbaks. – I will be back soon.

277 There is one single use-case where addressing one person by *ni* is common and perfectly normal: when addressing employees in a store. In this case the whole workforce at the store or the company is referred to as a group.

▷ **168, the "polite" pronoun**

Säljer ni frimärken här? – Do you sell stamps here?

---

[7] *Tills* is originally a contraction of *till dess* (until) and is not to be seen as synonymous to the directional *till* in this case.

[8] Mostly used in negated sentences.

Har ni öppet imorgon? – Are you open tomorrow?

278 In Swedish, *du* can be used as a conversation starter to get someone's attention, similarly to using *hey* or someone's name in English.

Du, får jag låna en penna? – Hey, can I borrow a pen?

Du? Jag älskar dig. – Honey? I love you.

Du, smöret är slut. – Hey, we're out of butter.

279 An even more informal way to address someone or to get someone's attention is using the term *hörrö/hörru*[9]. It's a contraction of *hör* (hear) and *du* (you).

Lägg av, hörrö! – Hey! Cut it out!

Hörrö! Du tappade något! – Hey! You dropped something!

Hörrö, vill du följa med? – Hey, do you want to tag along?

Hörrö du, du! – Hey, you!
(What are you doing!?)

Related to this expression, there is also *sörrö/serru* from *ser* (see) and *du*. Both *hörrö* and *sörrö* can be used as a filler, equivalent to *well you know*. Depending on the intonation, this can sound quite aggressive. Beware!

---

[9] Don't ask me why, but I would, personally, rather say *hörru/serru* but type it out as *hörrö/sörrö*. This is strictly spoken Swedish anyway.

Jo, hörrö/sörrö, jag var tvungen. – Yeah, well, you know, I had to.

Så här gör man, hörrö/sörrö. – See, this is how you do it.

Man får inte vara dum, hörrö/sörrö. – One mustn't be stupid, you know.

To my ear, *hörrö* sounds stronger and more directed towards the listener.

When addressing more than one person, there is also the plural equivalent *hörni* (*hör* + *ni*).

280 *Älvdalska* (Dalecarlian[10], Elfdalian) is a Swedish dialect (or rather a Norse language) spoken in the region of *Dalarna*. It is not officially seen as its own language by Swedish authorities but it's incomprehensible to people who didn't grow up with Elfdalian.

It has retained traits only found in Old Norse. Traits that Swedish and most other Scandinavian languages have lost: e.g. personal verb conjugations, masculine and feminine gender, dative and accusative, etc.

Mentioning this is a bit out of the scope of this book, but learners frequently ask about this and since this book is supposed to have all the answers – well...

281 There's lots of talk about how Scandinavian languages are

---

[10] From the word *dalkarl* (male person from *Dalarna*).

really one big dialect continuum and how intelligible they are among each other. It's true but this needs clarifying.

The languages drifted apart into dialects. However only the actual national borders (and thus the national school and media) have kept the languages, which can sound quite similar in the border regions, separated from each other. Furthermore, due to different unions and modern globalization, the languages have influenced each other somewhat further.

This means that, with Swedish in the backpack, Norwegian and Danish[11] can, with different amounts of effort, be quite comprehensible.

The following example will show you just how similar the languages can be. The examples are in the following order: Swedish, Danish, Norwegian *bokmål*, Norwegian *nynorsk*, and English:

Jag	sitter	och	läser	en	bok
Jeg	sidder	og	læser	en	bog
Jeg	sitter	og	leser	en	bok
Eg	sit	og	lesar	ein	bok
I am	sitting	and	reading	a	book

[11] Icelandic not so much.

As you can see, in terms of written Scandinavian, reading a book in these languages would actually require little effort. At the most, it could be done using a dictionary now and then. In a basic example like this, even Icelandic would be understandable (being similar to *nynorsk* in this case), but due to the huge amount of newly created words (and lack of loans) and preservation of grammatical cases, it becomes difficult to read really fast.

Before moving on, it's important to know that where the Swedish alphabet has *å*, *ä*, and *ö*, Danish and Norwegian use *æ*, *ø*, *å* (yes, they changed the order).

282 Norwegian is, together with Icelandic and Faroese, a West Scandinavian language that in reality is more similar to Swedish and Danish, which belong to the East Scandinavian branch. It has two pitch accents, similar to Swedish, but also (one of) its written language (*bokmål*) is heavily influenced by Danish. This makes the language (or rather, certain dialects) very easily understood by Swedes.

The other official written Norwegian standard is called *nynorsk* (new Norwegian) which emerged as a response to the heavily Danish influenced Norwegian during the Danish-Norwegian union era. It is based on south-western rural dialects and is more difficult for a Swede to understand.

Ultimately this means that those dialects that are closer to written *bokmål* are much easier to understand than the dialects that *nynorsk* is based on.

283 Danish is the only language that exists within the same language branch as Swedish but is, oddly, also the one that takes the most effort for a Swede to understand. This is because the pronunciation[12] has developed in an entirely different way than Swedish. Furthermore, even if Swedish has a bunch of German loans, Danish has another set of German loans that Swedes don't understand. However, since the languages are the closest related among the Scandinavian languages, intelligibility will come with enough exposure.

The reason for Danish pronunciation being so different from the northern siblings is the amount of reduced sounds – something the learner of Swedish is familiar with. However, the Danes have gone a step further, making the need for some initial exposure essential before understanding an iota.

Consonants and vowels after a stressed vowel are mostly dropped or heavily reduced, making a word like *kage* (cake) pronounced something like /kæj/ or /kæe/. This is no big deal after some practice.

Danish also lacks the pitch accents that Swedish and Norwegian have, but has developed a glottal stop in its stead to differentiate between words. This as well as the special /dh/ [ð] at the end of words (e.g. *ud* (out) [uð]) highly likely gave rise to the hot potato metaphor.

284 No, Finnish is not a part of the Scandinavian (North

---

[12] Often compared to speaking with a hot potato inside one's mouth.

Germanic) language branch. It is a Fenno-Ugric language related to Estonian and, more distantly, to the Sami languages.

Finnish does, however, have thousands of Swedish loans, as well as a bunch of Old Norse and Proto-Germanic loan words. Some are direct loans and some are direct translations.

Finland-Swedish

285   A topic that is often overlooked in books aimed towards learners of Swedish is the language spoken in Finland. No, I'm not talking about Finnish.

Finland-Swedish, or Fenno-Swedish, refers to the rather genuine eastern Swedish dialects as well as the official standard spoken in the former eastern half of Sweden which today is the Republic of Finland. A minority of Finlanders[1] speak Swedish as a native language and several counties are either bilingual or solely Swedish speaking.

I, the author, shouldn't assume that everyone learning Swedish is doing so because of a future in Sweden or because of Swedish friends, Swedish partners or Swedish ancestry. Maybe some of you out there are actually gazing upon the land of a thousand lakes. This chapter is dedicated to you.

286   Before moving on to differences and quirks of Finland-Swedish, it's worth mentioning that the Åland Islands (Finnish *Ahvenanmaa*) is an autonomous region that culturally has its own identity and also differs linguistically from Finland-Swedish. The closeness to Sweden, and the cultural distance from the Finland-Swedish culture has kept the language there closer to the dialects spoken on the east

---

[1] Citizens of Finland, as opposed to Finns who are **Finnish speaking** Finlanders.

coast of modern Sweden and the inland region of *Dalarna* and will not be a subject of this chapter.

Worth noting when talking about accents however is that eastern Ålandian Swedish sounds closer to the nearby mainland Finland-Swedish.

287 Swedish citizens often confuse Finland-Swedish wrongly as Swedish with a Finnish accent. There is however a big variety of accents in Finland and although some dialects, foremost the standard high Swedish (*högsvenska*[2]), have been influenced by Finnish over the years in terms of prosody and vocabulary, a Finn speaking Swedish with an accent will show a bunch of additional traits. This includes the wrong use of stress and lack of voiced consonants, aspiration, the lack of both *sje* and *tje* sounds (replacing those with /s/), and so on.

Since the Finn will most certainly have learned the Finland-Swedish standard accent in school, this helps spread the illusion among Swedes that this particular accent must be broken Swedish.

288 Standard Finland-Swedish is curated by Kotus[3] which somewhat tries to keep the language to not drift too far away from a common Swedish norm. However the genuine dialects can turn out to be rather incomprehensible to a Swede.

---

[2] *Högsvenska* is school Swedish based on the Helsinki pronunciation.

[3] Kotimaisten kielten keskus (Institute of the languages of Finland)

289 Where Sweden-Swedish has a quite complicated palette of vowels, Finland-Swedish has a far more reduced vowel spectrum.

a [a, a:]	tappa [tap:a] (to drop)	apa [a:p:a] (monkey)
o [u, u:]	dom [dum:] (sentence)	stor [stu:r] (big)
o [o, o:]	boll [bol:] (ball)	sova [so:va] (to sleep)
u [ʉ, ʉ:]	full [fʉl:] (full)	hus [hʉ:s] (house)
å [o, o:]	fånge [fɔŋ:e] (prisoner)	sås [so:s] (sauce)
e [e, e:]	elva [el:va] (eleven)	leka [le:k:a] (to play)
e [æ]	herre [hær:e] (gentleman)	–
i [i, i:]	lista [lis:ta] (list)	is [i:s] (ice)
y [y, y:]	sylt [syl:t] (jam)	yla [y:la] (to howl)
ä [e, e:]	ägg [eg:] (egg)	äga [e:ga] (to own)
ä [æ, æ:]	ärr [ær:] (scar)	lärare [læ:rare] (teacher)
ö [ø, ø:]	öster [øs:tær] (East)	öga [ø:ga] (eye)

ö [œ, œː]   förr [fœːr] (before)   höra [hœːra] (to hear)

If you remember, the long vowels in Sweden-Swedish usually have different qualities depending on whether they're long or short. In Finland-Swedish, there is only one quality for both lengths.

290 The feared *sje* sound does not exist in Finland-Swedish. Instead it is pronounced as a lighter sounding *tje* sound. Words with an original *tje* sound are pronounced with an initial *t-*.

kök /t-tjöööök/ – kitchen

sjuk /tjuuuuk/ – sick

291 In standard Finland-Swedish, *r* is trilled and is not usually a flap. However, dialectal variations of this letter also exist in Finland.

292 Finland-Swedish traditionally officially lacks retroflex consonants, at least in the standard language but they have started to pop up more frequently lately in news broadcasts. Something is a-happening.
▷ **82, retroflex consonants**

293 The consonant combination *dj-* is pronounced /dj/ as opposed to in Sweden where the *d-* is omitted.
▷ **86, the *j* sound**

294 Standard Finland-Swedish totally lacks the characteristic pitch accent as goes for almost all dialects in Finland.

295 The genuine dialects lack the quantity rule and have kept the Old Norse possibility of keeping a short vowel in front of a short consonant or a long vowel in front of a long consonant. Since this is possible also in Finnish, this enhances the illusion of Finland-Swedish being broken Swedish.

There are also cases where this happens in standard pronunciation although language authorities have recommended keeping the quantity rule in formal and official settings.

296 The Finland-Swedish standard accent has been said to be easier for learners to understand due to the lack of reductions (foremost in word boundaries), as opposed to Sweden-Swedish where everything ends up sounding like one single word.

297 *Inte* (not), *skulle* (would), and *redan* (already) are commonly reduced to *int*, *sku*, and *ren* which can sound archaic and particularly rural to a Swede.

298 While *dom* (they) is gaining popularity also in Finland, it's still more common to use the written forms *de* and *dem* in speech as well. They are then often pronounced /di/ and /dem/.

299 There is this issue as old as time in Finland-Swedish where an extra *att* (that) is shoved in front of the verb of a sentence, when the subject is separated from it by another clause.

Det tycker jag är bra. – I think that's good.
(Sweden, lit. "That, I think, is good.")

Det tycker jag att är bra. – I think that's good.
(Finland, lit. "That, I think, that is good.")

This sounds outright wrong to a Swede and is also regarded as an error by language regulators.

300 *Nog*, which is used to express uncertainty in Swedish, means the opposite in Finland and can be translated to *definitely* instead.

▷ **263, *nog***

Jag ska nog gå. – I think I might go.
(Sweden)

Jag ska nog gå. – I'll definitely go.
(Finland)

301 Addressing people with *ni* is not as problematic in Finland as it is in Sweden and lacks the same undertone as discussed in an earlier chapter.

▷ **168, the "polite" pronoun**

302 Due to the influence of the Finnish *vaikka* (although), Finland-Swedish has the rather peculiar direct translation (*fast*) which has gotten additional meanings added that generally don't exist in Swedish: *incredibly*, *for instance*, *if that's the case*, etc.

Filmen är fast hur kiva[4]! – The movie is incredibly good!

Vi kan fara[5] fast till Åbo. – We could go to Turku for instance.

Jag kan ta fast[6] bussen. – I could take the bus if that's the case.

This is incomprehensible to a Swede, who would assume that *fast* means *although, solid, fixed, stuck,* etc.

Some common Swedish expressions, understood by all speakers, are *som helst, till exempel, om det är så,* etc.

Filmen är hur bra som helst! – The movie is incredibly good!

Vi kan åka till Åbo till exempel. – We could go to Turku for instance.

Jag kan ta bussen om det är så. – I can take the bus if that's the case.

303 When a Swede wants to refer to a recent point in time, it is done with the preposition *i.* The Finland-Swede, however, uses *på* instead.
▷ **117, *på***

---

[4] *Kiva* is a loan from Finnish meaning *nice, good* or *fun.*

[5] In Sweden, *åka* is more often preferred over *fara* except for certain expressions and particle verbs.

[6] A Swede would read this as the particle verb *ta fast* which means *to capture.*

Sweden	Finland
i lördags (last saturday)	på lördagen
i natt (last night)	på natten

Swedes would expect more context to go with *på lördagen* or *på natten* and would just ask themselves *which Saturday* and *which night*.

304 The expression *som bäst* means that something is at its best when a condition is met.

Vintern är som bäst när det snöar. – The winter is at its best when it snows.

It is also commonly used to mean *to be in the middle of doing something the most intensely*.

När vi jobbade som bäst gick strömmen. – When we were working away the power went out.

In Finland, however, it can also mean *right now*, which can startle a Swede and cause misunderstandings.

Jag håller på som bäst att äta. – I'm eating right now.

305 A provincial vocabulary is nothing uncommon but it starts getting a bit special when a language is spoken in different countries. Finland-Swedish has a rich vocabulary that differs from that in Sweden and that Swedes might have trouble understanding.

Some words are loans from Finnish, some are archaic expressions that the Swede might not know or commonly use anymore, and some are just unique creations and compounds that don't exist in Sweden.

I've put together a small list with examples of this. It's by no means a complete list nor is it free of regional and colloquial expressions that aren't used in standard Swedish or by every Swedish speaking Finlander but it gives you an overview of the vast variety in vocabulary for a diverse number of topics.

Finland	Sweden
hoppeligen (hopefully)	förhoppningsvis
farmare (jeans)	jeans
paff[7] (cardboard, paper)	papp
rosk (trash)	skräp, sopor
krabbis (hangover)	bakfylla
dynvar (pillowcase)	örngott
roskis (trashcan)	soptunna/papperskorg
småkusin (second cousin)	syssling
simma[8]	bada

---

[7] *Paff* means *taken aback* in Sweden.

[8] You can see why this is confusing to a Swede. ▷ **215, *simma, bada***

skyddsväg (pedestrian crossing)	övergångsställe
semla (bread roll)	fralla/småfranska/bulle
gå på länk (to take a walk)	gå på promenad
kaveri (friend)	vän, kompis
ämbar[9] (bucket)	hink
T-skjorta (t-shirt)	T-shirt/T-tröja
örfil[10] (cinnamon bun)	kanelbulle
kiva (nice, good, fun)	trevlig, bra, kul
egnahemshus (one-family house)	villa
villa (summer house)	sommarstuga
håsa (to hurry, to do something quick and sloppy)	skynda, slarva
paja[11] (to pet)	klappa

---

[9] This word is pretty unusual in Sweden.

[10] Direct translation from Finnish *korvapuusti* which means *slap* but can also refer to a *cinnamon bun*. Totally incomprehensible to a Swede who would think it means *slap*.

[11] In Sweden *paja* is colloquial for breaking something.

julgubben (Santa Claus)	jultomten
råddig (untidy)	stökig
tråtta (to cram)	pressa
kila (to cut in line)	tränga sig före
verrare (sweatpants)	mjukisbyxor
söndra (to break)	ha sönder
idas[12] (to feel like/have the energy to do something)	orka
byk[13] (laundry)	tvätt
vessa (toilet)	toalett
barnträdgård (kindergarten)	förskola, dagis
acku (rechargeable battery)	(uppladdningsbart) batteri
skrinna[14] (to skate)	åka skridskor
juttu (thing, story)	sak/grej, historia

[12] Seldom used in Sweden nowadays.
[13] If a Swede knows this word, it's as an archaic expression.
[14] Finland – Where expressions go to die.

Notes & Acknowledgements

Since my early teens (as far as I can remember), I've been wanting to write and publish books. The written word amazes me and intrigues me. It is one of mankind's most extraordinary inventions by far and together with the invention of the bookpress some 500 years ago, ideas, instructions, and stories could suddenly be shared in the thousands. Being able to read is a gift too many take for granted and on top of that, having the privilege to read in several languages is a power that transcends everything.

With this book, I want to contribute to this cultural treasure and record my ever-changing native language as it is today in 2021 while giving the learners of Swedish the tools to understand why something is and the tools to decipher more dated texts. It also gives me the opportunity to finally cross something off my bucket list.

I'm humble enough to realize that this book could not have seen the light of day with only my own efforts and I think a few *thank yous* are in order. A big thank you to *mamma* and *pappa* for always supporting my (sometimes) unordinary interests and for letting me walk my own path in life, to my *livskamrat* Aniko for enduring not only me but also my sometimes philosophical and rhetorical linguistic questions, and to my bilingual *barn* Teodor and Ida, who give me thrilling insights in how language is acquired and how children handle two languages at the same time. I also want to thank my language teachers in school, who had to endure difficult questioning and, sometimes, corrections. If you, against all odds, are reading this book: my sincere apologies. At least a few apologies.

This book wouldn't have been half as good without the awesome work and help from my friends and community. A huge thank you to Elizabeth for making sure my English is on point, and to Christoph, Emre, Manuel, Mikael, Moritz, Pasi, Tobias, and Victoria for finding all sorts of errors and giving me good suggestions on improving this book. Much love to you all.

Tack så himla mycket.

Sources

Barnes, Michael. 2008. *A new introduction to Old Norse*. 3rd ed.
London: University College London.

Bäckström, Linnéa. 2020. *Vi kan både ha och mista ha*.
https://spraktidningen.se/2020/04/vi-kan-bade-ha-och-mista-ha/
(Accessed 7 July 2021)

Haugen, Einar. 1984. *Die skandinavischen Sprachen*. Hamburg:
Helmut Buske Verlag Hamburg.

Holmes, Philip; Hinchliffe, Ian. 2013. *Swedish: A Comprehensive
Grammar*. 3rd ed. Abingdon: Routledge.

Hultman, Tor G. 2003. *Svenska Akademiens språklära*. Stockholm:
Svenska Akademien.

Hällström-Reijonen, Charlotta. 2013. *Att va? Om den
finlandssvenska satsflätan*. https://www.sprakbruk.fi/-/att-va-om-
den-finlandssvenska-satsflatan (Accessed 25 June 2021)

Institutet för språk och folkminnen. *När använder man från
respektive ifrån?*. https://www4.isof.se/cgi-bin/srfl/visasvar.py?
sok=ifr%C3%A5n&svar=37158&log_id=815127 (Accessed 25 June
2021)

Institutet för språk och folkminnen. *När ska man använda av och när utav?*. https://www4.isof.se/cgi-bin/srfl/visasvar.py? sok=utav&svar=48426&log_id=815128 (Accessed 25 June 2021)

Institutet för språk och folkminnen. *Vilket är rätt: min blå klänning eller min blåa klänning?*. https://www4.isof.se/cgi-bin/srfl/visasvar.py?sok=bl%C3%A5&svar=31750&log_id=815130 (Accessed 24 June 2021)

Institutet för språk och folkminnen. *Vad är det för skillnad på dens och dess?*. https://www4.isof.se/cgi-bin/srfl/visasvar.py?sok=%%% %&svar=48057&log_id=729358 (Accessed 4 July 2021)

Kotsinas, Ulla-Britt. 2003. *En bok om slang, typ*. Stockholm: Nordstedts Ordbok.

Leinonen, Therese. 2010. *An Acoustic Analysis of Vowel Pronunciation in Swedish Dialects*. Groningen: Rijksuniversiteit Groningen.

Pihl, Anne; Tegsveden Deveaux, Sofi. *Working in Sweden The A–Z Guide*. 2nd ed. Umeå: LYS.

Ramge, Britta. 2007. *Praktische Grammatik der schwedischen Sprache*. 2nd ed. Wilhelmsfeld: Gottfried Egert Verlag.

Reuter, Mikael. 1993. *Kortstavigt uttal*. https://www.sprakinstitutet.fi/sv/publikationer/sprakspalter/reuter

s_rutor_1986_2013/1993/kortstavigt_uttal (Accessed 22 June 2021)

Reuter, Mikael. 2011. *Vad gör du som bäst?*. https://www.sprakinstitutet.fi/sv/publikationer/sprakspalter/reuter s_rutor_1986_2013/2011/vad_gor_du_som_bast (Accessed 15 July 2021)

Reuter, Mikael. 2015. *Vokalerna i finlandssvenskan*. Helsingfors: Svenska litteratursällskapet i Finland.

Riad, Tomas. 1997. *Svenskt fonologikompendium*.

Svenska Akademiens ordböcker. https://svenska.se/ (Accessed 15 July 2021)

Svensson, Anders. 2020. *Så dogo svenskans pluralformer*. https://spraktidningen.se/2020/09/sa-dogo-svenskans-pluralformer/ (Accessed 22 June 2021)

Tandefelt, Marika. 2019. *Finländsk svenska från 1860 till nutid*. Helsingfors: Svenska litteratursällskapet i Finland.

Teleman, Ulf; Hellberg, Staffan, and Andersson, Erik. 1999. *Svenska Akademiens grammatik*. Stockholm: Svenska Akademien.

Wenner, Lena. 2010. *När lögnare blir lugnare*. Uppsala: Uppsala universitet.

Index

accent I & II 92, 93
accusative 150, 155, 156, 163, 280
acute accent 92, 93
adjectives 5, 42–49
adverbs 51–54, 119–122
alltså 53, 272
andra 62, 66, 153
annan 153
antingen eller 216
apropå 173
aspiration 87
assimilation 104
asså 272
att 109, 299
att bero på 173
bada 215
bankomat 222
biff rule 144
blunda 221
bonusfamilj 209
bonusmamma 209
bonuspappa 209
borde 133
bra 237
betyda 239
buzzing *i* 71
båda 236
både och 236

bägge 236
böra 133
centuries 241
compounds 19, 234
compressed *i* 71
conjunctions 63
consonants 78–88
Dalecarlian 280
Danish 281, 283
dative 155, 164, 280
de/dem 57, 107, 298
definite form 1, 4, 5, 13
demonstrative pronouns 61, 125
deponent verbs 35–37
det 125, 127
det bero på 173
determinative pronouns 125
diminutive 240
diphthongs 75
dom 107, 298
double consonants 90
double definite form 5
duktig 220
dålig 205
därför att 226
é 247
eftersom 171, 225
eftersom att 171

234

Elfdalian 280
eller (hur) 265, 267
en/ett 3, 123
farbror 208
farfar 208
farmor 208
fast 166, 302
few 62, 169
filler words 262–264, 272–274
Finland-Swedish 285–305
Finnish 284
fjäll 222
flicka 187
flickvän 210
folk 203
fort 214
future tense 28–31
få 132, 169
för (att) 227–229
före 167
förrän(s) 276
g 84, 85
gapa 221
genitive 17, 18, 154
gilla 198
glömma (bort) 212
god 237
godare 237
godast 237
gôtt 73
grave accent 92, 93

gå 183
ha 26, 27, 128
handla 199
heller 53, 146
hemtjänst 222
het 194
heta 238
helper verbs 39
hinna 39, 221
hörrö 279
hörru 279
i 71, 118
i svenska 242
-ig 99
ihjäl 185
illa 205, 207
indefinite form 1, 3
innan 167
inte 144
-is 245
-iskt 100
j 84–86, 293
ju 262
juice 189
k 84
kaka 188
kanske 81
kex 84, 188
kille 187
killkompis 210
komma (att) 28, 30

komma ihåg 211
känna (till) 240
köpa 199
kör 204
köra 204
leka 186
ligga 138
lite 169
liten 151, 196
little 169
long consonants 90
långsam(t) 214
lägga 139
lära (sig) 184
many 169
medan(s) 276
mena 239
minnas 211
morbror 209
morfar 209
mormor 209
much 169
mycket 169
många 169
människa 201
nakna substantiv 16
Ni 168, 277, 301
nog 263, 300
nouns 1–19, 97, 98, 110, 123–126, 162, 244–246
Norwegian 281, 282

numbers 65, 66
nämen 254
-*o* 246
ô 73
och 63, 109
också 53, 146
oj 254
ond 205
ordinal numbers 66
orka 221
panta 221
participle 49, 50, 258, 260
particle verbs 38
passa på 219
passive voice 34, 258, 259
past tense 25–27, 101, 115, 135, 137, 140
past participle 50
past perfect 27
perfect 26
person 202
pitch accents 92, 93
plastmamma 209
plastpappa 209
please 175–180
plural 6–13
pojke 187
pojkvän 210
polite Swedish 175–182
possessive case 17, 18, 154
possessive pronouns 43, 58, 60, 172,

261, 269

Posten 222

preposition 18, 55, 56, 116–122

present continuous 37, 117, 260, 268

present participle 49, 260

pronouns 57–62, 107, 168, 298

prosody 91

prova 190

pröva 190

på 117

på svenska 242

quantity rule 77, 89, 295

question tags 264, 265–267

r 83, 291

reductions 94–113, 296

reflexive pronouns 59, 60

reflexive verbs 32, 33

retroflex consonants 82, 292

riksdagen 222

rån 188

saft 189

sambo 209

senast(e) 200

serru 279

simma 215

sist(a) 200

sitta 138, 268

sje sound 81, 287, 290

ska 24, 28, 29, 39, 131, 256

Skatteverket 222

skola 24, 28, 29, 39, 41, 131, 177, 256

skulle 24, 41, 131, 177, 256

slang words 245, 246

slippa 221

små 151, 196

smärre 196

snabb(t) 104, 214

snusa 221

snälla 178

soft *g* 84–86

soft *k* 84

som 129

spela 186

spendera 195

stress 89–91

strong verbs 23, 140, 161

styvfar 209

styvmamma 209

styvmor 209

styvpappa 209

stå 137, 268

ställa 139

subjunctions 64, 225–228

subjunctive mood 40, 41

subordinate clauses 64

Systembolaget 222

sämre 205

sämst 205

särbo 209

sätta 139

sörrö 279

tack 176

temporal expressions 117, 118, 303

tenth vowel 73

till 154, 230, 276

tillbaka 276

tillbaks 276

tills 276

tillbringa 195

timma 197

timme 197

tje sound 80, 287, 290

tjej 187

tjejkompis 210

tjockt l 88

tjôta 73

trapp 197

trappa 197

tro 193

trivas 218

tycka 192

tycka om 198

tänka 28, 31, 191

uncountable nouns 14, 15

V2 223

va 266

vabba 222

vobba 222

vowels 68–76, 289

var(t) 165

vare sig eller 216, 215

varken eller 216, 215

varmt 194

vaska 221

verbs 20–41

Viby-i 71

vårdcentral 222

vårt avlånga land 222

väl 264

vänligen 179

värre 206, 207

värst 206, 207

word order 144, 223

å 69, 70, 75, 109, 157

åt 231

Åland Islands 286

ä 69, 70, 75

älv 222

Älvdalska 280

ända 197

ände 197

är 108

även fast 166

även om 166

ö 69, 70, 74, 75

Printed in Great Britain
by Amazon